T0277197

UNITAS TO UNITAS

Unitas to Unitas

Life's Lessons Passed Down from Father to Son

Joe Unitas

As Told to Kristine Setting Clark

Forewords by Joe Namath and Dan Fouts

LYONS
PRESS

Essex, Connecticut

An imprint of The Globe Pequot Publishing Group, Inc.
64 South Main Street
Essex, CT 06426
www.globepequot.com

Distributed by NATIONAL BOOK NETWORK

British Library Cataloguing in Publication Information available

Library of Congress Cataloging-in-Publication Data
Names: Unitas, Joe, 1974- author. | Clark, Kristine Setting, 1950- author. |
    Namath, Joe Willie, 1943- author of foreword. | Fouts, Dan, 1951 author of
    foreword.
Title: Unitas to Unitas : life's lessons passed down from father to son / Joe Unitas,
    as told to Kristine Setting Clark ; forewords by Joe Namath and Dan Fouts.
Description: Essex, Connecticut : Lyons Press, [2025] | Includes bibliographical
    references.
Identifiers: LCCN 2024022581 (print) | LCCN 2024022582 (ebook) | ISBN
    9781493086023 (hardcover ; acid-free paper) | ISBN 9781493086030 (e-book)
Subjects: LCSH: Unitas, Joe, 1974- | Unitas, Johnny, 1933-2002—Family. |
    Actors—United States—Biography. | Conduct of life.
Classification: LCC PN2287.U56 A3 2025 (print) | LCC PN2287.U56 (ebook) |
    DDC 791.4302/8092 [B]—dc23/eng/20240708
LC record available at https://lccn.loc.gov/2024022581
LC ebook record available at https://lccn.loc.gov/2024022582

♾️™ The paper used in this publication meets the minimum requirements of
American National Standard for Information Sciences—Permanence of Paper for
Printed Library Materials, ANSI/NISO Z39.48-1992.

To Dianna, Clark, Colten, and Casey.
You all make me strive to be better.

Contents

Foreword by Joe Namath ix

Foreword by Dan Fouts xi

Introduction xiii

First Quarter: My Dad, My Hero **1**

Life's Lesson #1: It Doesn't Cost Anything to Be Nice 5

Life's Lesson #2: Be Tough! 9

Life's Lesson #3: Know the Difference between
Right and Wrong 13

Life's Lesson #4: Be There for Your Children 15

Life's Lesson #5: Be Disciplined. 19

Life's Lesson #6: Don't Lie! 23

Life's Lesson #7: Be a Good Teammate 25

Life's Lesson #8: Winning Is All That Matters 29

Second Quarter: The Winds of Change. **31**

Life's Lesson #9: Be 100 Percent Committed 33

Life's Lesson #10: Support and Make Time for
Your Children 37

Life's Lesson #11: Don't Quit 39

Life's Lesson #12: Working Hard Pays Off 43

Life's Lesson #13: Be Your Own Person and Be Judged as Such 45

Life's Lesson #14: Discipline and Structure Are Key Factors. 49

Life's Lesson #15: Don't Dismiss Any Dream as Too Big. 51

Life's Lesson #16: One-on-One Time Is Important .59

Life's Lesson #17: You Have to Let Go 63

Third Quarter: Hollywood and the Stars 67
Life's Lesson #18: Believe in Yourself, Because If You Don't, No One Else Will 69

Fourth Quarter: Adulthood: Love, Marriage, Family, and Responsibility 91
Life's Lesson #19: There Is Nothing More Important than Family. 97

Life's Lesson #20: Be a Leader and Not a Follower 103

Overtime: A Tribute to Dad 131

Acknowledgments 155

References 159

About the Authors 161

Foreword by Joe Namath

When you talk about 1950s and early '60s football, Johnny Unitas was the man. Just look at that haircut and those black high-tops. To look at him, physically, he didn't look that tough, but he *was* that tough. His teammates knew it because of his leadership and how he conducted himself on the field. Unlike today, Unitas also called his own plays and was very unpredictable. He was a defensive player's worst nightmare. To me, he epitomized what a gridiron general should be.

Western Pennsylvania is where both John and I grew up. During the 1940s and '50s, many people in that area were employed by either the steel mills or the coal mines. Becoming an athlete was one of the few ways to escape the toxic exposure of the mills and the mines. Johnny Unitas had been my football hero since I was a little kid back in Beaver Falls, Pennsylvania. He had the instincts, the desire, and the toughness that I one day hoped to achieve. Whenever I watched him play, I became so inspired; I even wore number 19 in high school and was nicknamed "Joey U." I wanted to do everything he did . . . I wanted to *be* him.

There was also a guy from our hometown by the name of Jim Mutscheller who played tight end for the Baltimore Colts. I immediately became a Colts fan. In 1969 when the Jets played the Baltimore Colts in Super Bowl III, it was like a dream come true for me. And when I met Johnny Unitas, personally, it was the ultimate experience, to meet my idol.

Earl Morrall started that game because John had been hurt for most of the season. But when Unitas came onto the field—even though we were ahead—I promise you, I looked up at that clock and said, "Please God, run that clock." I never asked the Good Lord for us to come out ahead or anything like that, but when John stepped on the field, any defense that played against him knew he had the ability to lead his team back to victory. His presence alone would leave you on edge.

Unitas came in and marched the Colts 80 yards to a touchdown with 3:19 still left in the game. The Colts lined up for an onside kick and recovered the ball, but it was too little, too late.

John was one of the toughest competitors and most determined guys I have ever met. The man was a tremendous football player, and one of the best quarterbacks to ever play the game.

—Joe Namath
New York Jets, 1965–76
Los Angeles Rams, 1977
Pro Football Hall of Fame, 1985

FOREWORD BY DAN FOUTS

As the son of the San Francisco 49ers broadcaster in the 1950s and '60s, Bob Fouts, I was a loyal and avid Niner fan. The team was loaded with future Hall of Fame members. Names like Y. A. Tittle, Hugh "The King" McElhenny, Joe "The Jet" Perry, John Henry Johnson, Leo "The Lion" Nomellini, Bob "The Geek" St. Clair, Jimmy Johnson, Dave Wilcox, and All-Pro quarterback John Brodie highlighted the roster. But, for as great as these players were, the 49ers could not get over the hump and win an NFL title. A quarterback for the Baltimore Colts named John Unitas always seemed to beat my beloved "Prospectors."

When I was sixteen, with my obvious connection to the 49ers, thanks to my dad, I was lucky enough to be a ball boy at Kezar Stadium during many of those games. Little did I know that in six short years, I would be sharing a locker room with the greatest quarterback that ever played, Johnny U.

John was traded to the San Diego Chargers in 1973 after seventeen tremendous seasons with the Colts. Earlier that off-season, I was drafted by San Diego. That was the beginning of an amazing opportunity for me to observe, learn from, and be awed by this amazing athlete and man. My only regret was that our time together was all too brief. Even though that span was cut short by injury, to John, I learned so much about playing the position that was beneficial throughout my own fifteen-year career. You could label them the "tricks of the trade." The timing of the drop back, the use of "looking off" the defense, reading the defense before the ball is snapped, and confirming your reads as you settled into the pocket.

Perhaps the coolest aspect of watching Johnny U was his presence on the field, in the locker room, in meetings, and, most importantly, in the huddle. He had *it*—an aura that breathed confidence, arrogance, toughness, strength, and competitiveness. It was my privilege and my honor to have such a special opportunity and relationship with the greatest of all time, John Unitas. Enjoy this unique and insightful look into the life and times of Johnny U as only a son could share.

—Dan Fouts
San Diego Chargers, 1973–87
Pro Football Hall of Fame, 1993

INTRODUCTION

Professional football in the 1950s captured an era when the sport really began to move forward into the new decade. America was now a mighty world power, and playing football was for tough, rugged, honest men who played primarily for the love of the game.

During the 1950s, pro football entered its marriage with television. Thanks to TV, the game was transported out of the backwaters of the American sports scene and thrust into the mainstream. With its unique way of capturing the spontaneity and immediacy of live events, television proved to be the perfect medium for pro football.

During this time, the NFL consisted of only twelve teams in eleven cities, with thirty-three players on each team. They played a twelve-game schedule for most of the decade. A total of seventy-two games were played throughout the entire NFL season.

The sport was about to make an imprint on America's consciousness, and for those just beginning to discover the NFL, it was love at first sight—thanks to a colorful collection of gridiron characters whose low salaries never dampened their high spirits. It was a time when $20,000 salaries were the exception, and $6,000 salaries were the rule. It was the last *pure* football, played by a select few.

Professional football's popularity grew by leaps and bounds. Per-game attendance increased in every year of the decade. Season ticket prices were around $20.00, and individual game tickets went for $4.00 and $5.00.

The 1958 NFL Championship Game between the Baltimore Colts and the New York Giants—considered by many to be *the greatest game ever played*—carried every element of football drama: great catches, unbelievable runs and goal-line stands, multiple turnovers, and eight quarterback sacks. There was even an NBC cable break that cut off transmission for several minutes, causing an emotional frenzy in millions of homes around the nation. It was fifty minutes of prelude that set the stage for an unforgettable finish—the first "sudden death" game in professional football history.

This gridiron event, which was watched nationally by over forty million people, is considered the foundation upon which the modern-day NFL was built.

John Unitas, the winning quarterback of that '58 Championship Game, was all that America wanted in a man in the 1950s. He was hardworking, humble, respectful, and true to his word. As a football player, Unitas became known for his trademark crew cut and black high-top cleats, which he would later wear when cutting grass because "they were comfortable and still fit."

Blessed with athleticism and a golden arm, he had a heart that pumped ice water through his veins, allowing him to remain unemotional in the tensest moments of football games. In fact, he is credited with *inventing—and perfecting—*the two-minute drill. But statistics and accolades weren't important to him, only winning.

As a child I wore out a VHS tape by NFL Films entitled *The NFL's Best Ever Quarterbacks.* In that video the narrator says, "While many quarterbacks have been compared to Unitas, Unitas has never been compared to anyone else." He simply set the standard for what quarterbacks are today.

My name is Joe Unitas, and I was fortunate enough to have had twenty-eight great years with my dad. I believe I know the essence of the man. His ambition, determination, and courage never wavered. He was the leader of our family. The examples he set and the lessons he taught are my dad's legacy to me. He was always my biggest supporter and the most incredible source of inspiration. His passion and motivation to be the best served as the foundation upon which many of my successes have been built.

I have taken his legacy a step further by writing this book about the life lessons my dad taught me and how they have served as a road map as I've pursued my goals. I offer deeply personal reflections on how I've applied these twenty lessons throughout my life, responding to situations differently as a child, then an adolescent, and later, as an adult.

But before I can begin my story of how my dad impacted my life, you will need to know the driving force behind his.

* * *

The year was 1933. It was one of the worst years of the Great Depression. Fifteen million Americans were unemployed. Al Capone ruled Chicago, and Hitler came into power in Germany. On a lighter note, Prohibition had ended, the film *King Kong* premiered, major league baseball's first All-Star Game was played, and the New York Giants beat the Washington Senators four games to three in the World Series. In the NFL, the Chicago Bears hosted the New York Giants at Wrigley Field in the league's inaugural Championship Game. The Bears edged by the Giants, 23–21, in front of 25,000 fans.

On May 7, 1933, John Constantine Unitas was born in the coal town of Pittsburgh, Pennsylvania. Dad was the son of Francis and Helen Unitas, the third of four children. According to my uncle Leonard, his older brother, my dad was the apple of his father's eye.

When my dad was just five years old, his father died of kidney failure, leaving his Lithuanian-born mother, Helen, to support the family. "Grams," the name I knew my grandmother by, was the stabilizing force in their lives. She lacked a formal education and, therefore, had to work three jobs just to make ends meet. In the early hours of the morning, she worked at a bakery. From there she transitioned to her day job, selling insurance, and in the evening, she cleaned offices. Grams had a compelling work ethic, and was known to say, "If you have to scrub toilets, make 'em shine." She had another saying that she used quite frequently with her children: "If you have a *need*, we will discuss it. If you have a *want*, don't bring it up."

At age eight, my dad found his passion for football, and his dream to become a professional player had begun. One day, while stirring the coal in the basement furnace (one of Dad's chores), he found an old tire and some rope, which he used to hang the tire from a tree limb in his yard. He spent countless hours trying to throw a football through the tire. Whenever possible, he would enlist his younger sister Shirley to push the tire back and forth so he could practice throwing to a moving target.

Dad was not a big guy. Upon graduating from high school, he was six feet tall, but very thin—about 135 pounds. Shirley, who was a cheerleader for St. Justin's, the high school she and Dad attended, was always scared when he would get tackled. It made her cringe because she didn't know if he was going to get up or not.

With the help of his high school coach and a St. Justin's priest, my dad was offered a tryout with Notre Dame. It was always his dream to play for the Fighting Irish. Although he performed well in the tryout, the coaches felt he was too small to play for their university and declined to offer him a scholarship. My dad applied to

Pitt and the University of Indiana, but was turned down due to mediocre grades.

In December 1950, my dad and Grams were visited by University of Louisville assistant football coach, Frank Gitschier. Prior to leaving U of L for the holiday, Frank had asked the current players if they knew of any high school players in western Pennsylvania that he should recruit. My dad's name was brought up.

During the in-home recruiting visit, Coach Gitschier not only promised Grams that if Dad came to U of L, Frank would make sure he graduated; he also promised that Dad would attend Mass every Sunday therein.

Upon returning to U of L in January, Frank found an envelope on his desk. Inside was a note from Grams, stating simply: "John wants to come."

Only five games into his freshman year, my dad was named the starting quarterback. By the time he graduated, he had passed for over 3,000 yards and 27 touchdowns. His dream to play in the NFL was about to become a reality.

After completing his senior season of football at Louisville in 1954, Dad returned to Pittsburgh for Thanksgiving vacation, where he married his high school sweetheart, Dorothy Jean Hoelle. Within the next year they had their first child, a girl, named Janice.

Dad was selected in the ninth round of the 1955 NFL draft by the Pittsburgh Steelers, but his time there would be short-lived, as head coach Walt Kiesling refused to play him. He was cut at the end of training camp, which was held at St. Bonaventure University in southwestern New York State, and told that management couldn't afford to carry three quarterbacks. My dad was furious. "I wouldn't mind getting cut," he told the coach. "That's not the problem—but you didn't even give me the opportunity!"

The Steelers gave him ten dollars for his bus fare home. He kept the ten and hitchhiked home instead. He needed the money for his wife and child, who were waiting for him in Pittsburgh.

My dad may have gotten cut by the Steelers, but he *knew* he was good, and that's the important part. He would show them all that they were wrong. His persistence was, once again, unmatched.

During that same year, my dad worked construction while playing defensive back and quarterback for a semi-pro team called the Bloomfield Rams. The Rams paid just six dollars a game and they played in horrific sandlot fields, lacking grass and covered in oil, to keep the dust down—not to mention all the broken glass scattered from one end of the field to the other. Finishing a game without the need for stitches was considered a win.

In late 1955 the Colts received a letter from a fan urging the team to consider my father. The team's general manager, Don Kellett, made an eighty-cent phone call to the wife of the Bloomfield Rams owner and asked if she could get a message to Dad about a tryout in Baltimore that coming spring. After the tryout, head coach Wilbur Charles "Weeb" Ewbank took a chance on this rawboned kid with the funny name and told him to come back for summer camp.

At the annual Blue–White scrimmage held during training camp, the announcers didn't even know how to properly pronounce his name. They called him John U-na-tass. Three games into the 1956 season, my dad replaced injured starter George Shaw. Although his first professional pass was intercepted and returned for a touchdown, Dad was there to stay. He would need only two years to turn a losing NFL team into champions. During his time in Baltimore the Colts were NFL champs in 1958, 1959, and 1968 (prior to the AFL–NFL merger), and they won Super Bowl V in 1971.

In 1973 my dad was traded to the San Diego Chargers, where a starting job and twice the salary awaited him. But at age thirty-nine, and due to injuries, he would only play five games. Football was changing, and my dad knew it. He retired at the end of the season.

He was the last of the pure quarterbacks. With continuous feedback from his offensive teammates, Dad called all the plays and made all the on-field decisions. He was one of the original "gridiron generals." His intelligence and toughness gained him respect from his peers, coaches, and fans alike throughout the nation. While he wasn't egotistical, he had total confidence in his ability to get the job done. *When you know what you're doing, you don't get intercepted.* He was always in charge on the field and trusted the other ten offensive players to execute the plays he called.

For the remainder of his life, he dealt with severe pain, but it never held him back. He stayed the course. He never changed who he was or tried to become someone he wasn't. He was sincere, but didn't get emotional over situations on the field. "I get emotional over kids and animals, not football games. I don't care about stats or records being broken—just winning."

Case in point: When the Colts moved to Indianapolis, my dad demanded that his records be taken out of the record book because he didn't play for the *Indianapolis* Colts, he played for the *Baltimore* Colts. Life was very simple to him: It was either black or white. There were very few gray areas. My father hated stupidity and couldn't stand thoughtless or out-of-line questions, especially from sportswriters. He would fire right back at them, saying, "I'm not going to answer that!" He had a memory like an elephant, and if you hurt him or invaded his privacy, the next time around you would get very little out of him in the way of a response. My dad wasn't big on socializing and kept pretty much to himself. Although he was actually a shy person, he was respected by all.

Dad passed away on September 11, 2002. At his funeral, he was eulogized by teammates, friends, and family. The tributes had very little to do with football. People spoke of my dad as more of a friend, a brother, and a father. The single thread that linked all of these remembrances together was that they spoke of Dad as a common man of uncommon talents, and even more, of uncommon grace. Over the years, without Dad even saying a word, I learned the important lesson of being humble simply by watching him.

My Dad, My Hero

It is the job of both a mother and a father to turn a boy into a man, but the major emphasis is often on the father. Throughout the ages it has been up to the father to instill in his son the importance of responsibility, accountability, kindness, confidence, hard work, and honor. Boys don't come with a set of instructions, and many of life's lessons are learned through hits and misses; but hopefully, there will be many more positive experiences than negative.

Young boys come into this world with unlimited love, curiosity, and energy. His journey toward becoming a man originates very early in life. It is the first time he looks at his dad and realizes, "I want to be just like him." And that's exactly how I felt about my dad.

I was born Francis Joseph Unitas (Francis, after my grandfather) to John and Sandy Unitas on March 24, 1974, in Baltimore, Maryland, the first of their three children. My brother, Chad Elliott, was born in 1978, followed by my sister, Alicia Ann Paige, in 1982. None of

Figure 1.1   With Dad in the locker room the day the Colts retired his famous number 19 in October 1977.

us were fortunate enough to see our dad play football, as he retired from the NFL in 1973.

My dad was always my most loyal and avid supporter. My close relationship with him began at a very young age. His character, values, and the kind of man he was would help to build the foundation for the man and father I am today.

Figure 1.2   Dad running off the field at Memorial Stadium after his jersey number was retired.

Life's Lesson #1

It Doesn't Cost Anything to Be Nice

ONE OF MY EARLIEST MEMORIES OF DAD WAS WHEN I realized how famous he was. Before that, I'd had no idea, because to me, he was just Dad. I was about five or six years old at the time. Quite often we would be driving in a car and people—total strangers—would be waving and calling out his name. At stoplights they would scream and freak out because they were so excited to see him. My dad always smiled and waved back. I would ask him if he knew these people, and he would answer with one word: "Nope." Although he was a man of few words, he always got his point across.

If he were walking down the street, people would stop him and ask for an autograph. He would always oblige. I once asked him why he accommodated their requests. "It doesn't cost anything to be nice," he replied." My dad learned early in his career that "being nice" was an extremely important part of his job.

My dad's rookie season with the Baltimore Colts was 1956. While in training camp, Commissioner Bert Bell visited the Colts, as he did with each NFL team, and talked to the players. He expressed to them the importance of their character both on and off the field. To the community they represented the Colts organization, and it was part of their job to mingle and be kind and accessible to the fans. After all, it was the fans who were paying the players' salaries.

Figure 1.3   At Canton for Dad's Hall of Fame induction, in 1979.

The Colts had their own marching band. In the late 1950s a member of the band, John Ziemann, was stricken on the field and rushed to the hospital with a ruptured appendix. Ziemann tells his story of what happened at the hospital following surgery: "I was in bed, tubes coming out of me, when one of the nurses said, 'Did you hear, Johnny Unitas is coming to see you?' I said, 'Yeah, right.' About two hours later, I looked up and there he was. Some of the band members told him what had happened. He took a picture with me and spent about two and a half hours talking with me about football. He gave me a game ball. I never forgot him for that."

Later in his career, my dad owned a restaurant in Baltimore. He named it the Golden Arm. I can remember many times having dinner with my dad or my family, and fans would walk up to the table and ask him for an autograph or to take a photo. Even if he was eating, he would stop and sign or pose for a picture. He enjoyed giving others happiness.

On a similar note, I once asked him, "What was the craziest thing you ever signed?" He said, "One woman asked me to sign her boobs." When I asked him what he did, he smiled and said, "I took my time and was sure to dot the 'i' and cross the 't.'" It doesn't cost anything to be nice, and I got paid back on this one!

Observing how my dad interacted with people in general taught me a great deal about how to act in a social environment.

Life's Lesson #2

Be Tough!

As children, we usually view our parents as "old" regardless of their age at the time. My dad was a child of the Depression era. He knew firsthand what it was like to live during tough times, an impact that would stay with him the rest of his life. But I never really knew how tough *he* was until the tractor mishap.

I used to love riding the tractor with my dad. We owned a large piece of property, and he really enjoyed the solitude that came with mowing the grass with the tractor. Dad had been a spokesperson for International Harvester tractors and had filmed some commercials for them. They, in turn, presented him with one of their tractors.

One day, my dad was working under the blades of the tractor, which were located between the front and back tires. He was lying on his back on the asphalt driveway next to our home, and I was sitting on the seat of the tractor while he was attempting to fix it.

For some reason my dad hadn't turned off the engine, leaving the tractor in neutral. While sitting on the seat—I was about seven years old at the time—I somehow hit the gearshift and the tractor began to move forward, with my dad still underneath the blades!

The tractor began to pick up speed and was now descending a small hill at the end of the driveway, heading toward the grass, about thirty to forty feet away. It slowed down as the descent gave way to a flat area, allowing my dad to break free from the treacherous blades. The tractor, with me still in the driver's seat, began to descend to the steep second level. At the bottom of the hill was a large tree.

Panicked, I jumped off the tractor just prior to it colliding with the massive trunk.

Once back on my feet, I ran to my dad, who was slowly getting up. Although he was badly bruised and cut, he walked down to the tractor and shut off the engine before we returned to the house.

It wasn't until I was much older that I was told this story about my dad breaking his nose during a game and not missing a down.

The Colts were playing the Bears. Defensive end Doug Atkins broke through the offensive line and hit my dad so hard that he broke his nose. The Colts called time-out, but even with all the gauze shoved up Dad's nose, they couldn't get the bleeding to stop. Finally, Colts offensive lineman Jim Parker grabbed some mud off the field and shoved it into his nose.

Coach Ewbank wanted to take him out of the game, but Dad said to Weeb, "If you even *try* to take me out of the game, I will fucking kill you."

On the next play he threw a touchdown pass.

Needless to say, my dad passed on his toughness to me. It wasn't as though I had a lot to say about it!

RUB SOME DIRT ON IT

As mentioned, our house was situated at the top of a hill. The driveway wound its way through the property, which was great for riding my dirt bike. One day my dad was on his tractor cutting the lawn on the lower section of our property. I was on my dirt bike and getting ready to pedal as fast as I could down the driveway. You could really pick up some serious speed! As I was flying down the hill, I passed my dad and continued to the grassy field, to slow down.

My dad had yet to cut that area, making it hard to see what was concealed beneath the tall, thick grass. I ended up hitting a six-inch-wide sewer pipe. Upon impact, I flew over the handlebars, landing on my right shoulder. I still had my shoulder pads on from lacrosse practice, but it didn't seem to cushion the fall. I just sat there on the ground, crying.

Because of the uneven landscape, my dad didn't see me right away. Once he did, he ran over to me, picked me up, and brought me back to the house. In the bathroom my dad lifted my arm up and down, rotating it clockwise and counterclockwise. When he was finished, he said, "See, you can still move it. You're fine."

I continued to cry. He told me that if it still hurt tomorrow, he would take me to the doctor.

The following morning the pain was still there, so Dad took me to see the doctor before school. X-rays showed that my collarbone was fractured, and my arm was immediately put into a sling. Now, at this point most parents would take their child home to rest their arm. Not my dad. He took me directly to school and said I would be fine. To add insult to injury, one of my classmates thought I was faking, so he punched me in the shoulder. That really hurt! The most disappointing part was that my lacrosse season was over.

My dad grew up in a generation that believed "rubbing a little dirt on it" would make everything okay. While this may not always be the case, there is one thing for sure: He made me a tougher person for it!

Life's Lesson #3

Know the Difference between Right and Wrong

"Eye of the Tiger"

The year was 1982. I was eight years old, and a member of the Hillendale Country Club swim team. We were attending a swim meet at the Eagle's Nest Country Club. Prior to the start of the meet, I walked into the locker room and noticed a cassette tape—the soundtrack to *Rocky III*, featuring "Eye of the Tiger"—sitting on the locker-room bench. It was one of my favorite songs, so I decided to take it.

I was taught never to steal, but this was different. It was "Eye of the Tiger," and it was *the* song of the day! I figured I could take it home and hide it from my parents. Now, the fact that I was eight years old shows you that I didn't put much thought into a hiding place. I hid the cassette in my parents' liquor cabinet, right next to Dad's Jack Daniel's.

One evening soon after, my parents were going out to a black-tie event. My dad found the tape and confronted me. "Where did you get this?" he said.

I immediately told him the pool locker room at Eagle's Nest. He, in turn, told my mom. They were already running late for their event, but that didn't matter to my dad. Right then and there he told me to get into the car and we drove directly to the club to return the tape—a twenty-minute ride each way. At the time, I thought he should have thanked me. (Black-tie events weren't at the top of his "fun things to do" list!)

When we arrived, my dad immediately took me to the manager's office to explain to him what I had done. That really shook me up. Obviously, I never did anything like that again.

Case in point: When my youngest son, Casey, was about four or five years old, we were at a crafts store. While I was purchasing some items, Casey was stealing a lollipop. As we got into the car, I heard him remove the plastic wrapper from the lollipop and I immediately turned off the engine. I asked him where he'd gotten the candy, and he remained very quiet.

I marched both he and his brother, Colten, back into the store. I told the manager that my son had something to tell him. This left an immediate impression on both of them. Even though my other son had done nothing wrong, I wanted him to experience what would happen if he did. The lesson I'd learned from my dad paid off with my own children.

Life's Lesson #4

Be There for Your Children

MY DAD ALWAYS HAD MY BACK

Baltimore is home to many remarkable schools in both the city and surrounding counties. Many of these schools are private. Their populations range from kindergarten through sixth grade to kindergarten through twelfth grade.

I attended Calvert School, one of the premier K–6 schools in Baltimore, for eight years. (The extra year will be explained shortly.) At the top of Calvert's administrative team was a headmaster by the name of Mr. Hall. Upon arriving at school each morning, students would climb up the front stairs, where they were greeted by the headmaster. From there, each student would have to look him in the eye, shake his hand, and say, "Good morning, Mr. Hall," after which the boys entered their designated wing of the building and the girls entered theirs.

Calvert did not implement the traditional grading system of A, B, C, D, and F. They utilized the numerical equivalent of 1, 2, 3, and 4. While most students were achieving 1s and 2s, I was underachieving, with 3s and 4s. But when it came to physical education, I *always* received a 1. That being said, I will explain why I spent eight years in a seven-year school.

As a six-year-old in kindergarten I spent more time walking the halls of the school than in the actual classroom. Academia and sitting still for long periods of time has been shown to create an unhealthy learning environment for many six-year-olds, especially boys. I know this because I was one of those students. Whenever I got bored or disinterested, which was often, I would say "I need to use the bathroom." Despite the fact that one bathroom's location was just outside the classroom door, I would usually opt to find one on the other side of the school. My immaturity and lack of focus forced me to repeat kindergarten, and thus, the extra year.

But my problems weren't over quite yet. Due to my low performance, my parents were eventually called in for a parent-teacher conference when I was in third grade. I wasn't exactly dazzling my math teacher with my skills, and she took the time to let my parents know exactly how she felt. I was in a remedial math class taught by the no-nonsense Ms. Cicil, a little old lady with white hair who walked with a cane and believed in strict enforcement of the rules.

As my parents sat down, she didn't pull any punches. "Your son can't make it here. I suggest you find a different school for him."

My dad let her know that under no circumstances would I be leaving Calvert (and for the record, I *did* graduate from Calvert in 1987). Education was *the* number one priority with him. He wasn't the best student, either, although his mother didn't have the financial means to get him additional academic support, like my parents did. They hired a math tutor to help me get through the remainder of that school year.

I continued to work with tutors throughout the majority of my school days. Over the years, we learned that I performed much better academically in smaller classes or one-on-one settings. For example, in my sophomore year I failed geometry despite working hard and asking the teacher for extra help. For some reason I just wasn't connecting with the teacher and the lessons. My parents went to bat for me and arranged for me to retake the class with a different teacher and in a one-on-one environment. This time everything clicked, and I got an A.

I can't remember a time when my parents weren't there to support me. Don't get me wrong—if I screwed up, my dad would be the first to let me know. But all in all, throughout the years, he always had my back.

Life's Lesson #5

Be Disciplined

D-I-S-C-I-P-L-I-N-E. I think I could spell this word before I could spell my own name. According to my dad, this was a cornerstone for success in anything you do. And he was 100 percent correct. Undisciplined people will fail in most endeavors.

I can recall numerous conversations about why I failed in various instances. Poor grades showed a lack of discipline in doing homework and/or studying. On the football field, poor discipline meant you hadn't watched film or studied your opponent, or focused enough in practice. My car being taken away was due to a lack of discipline in getting home by the set curfew time. Losing a game was quite often due to a lack of discipline in the team to work together as a unit. Being out of shape was due to lack of discipline in conditioning and in the weight room.

When it came to discipline, my dad was definitely old-school. Let's just say that terms like *time-out*, *psychological discipline techniques*, and *positive parenting* were not part of his vocabulary. Like many of his generation, grounding and corporal punishment were high on his list.

Most of my disciplinary experiences with my dad took place during elementary school. These prepubescent years were about learning right from wrong. When wrong trumped right, the consequences were usually delivered with a belt or a paddle of some sort. I also had my mouth washed out with soap a time or two. (Getting soap out of your teeth is quite the ordeal!)

Discipline wasn't always related to punishment. It also had to do with prioritizing your personal life. Time management is a big part of this. Prioritizing school, homework, and sports, not to mention keeping my room clean and organized, was a lot to ask of a teenager, but necessary. My dad was a big proponent of chores. According to him, chores were a form of discipline. In my dad's case, hard work was ingrained in him at a very early age.

"Just watching my mother, how hard she had to work for everything we had," my dad said, "was the greatest thing I ever saw. Sometimes I'd come home from a ball game, all beat up, and she'd say, 'You know Mrs. Wrigley up the street?' and I'd say, 'Yeah. I know Mrs. Wrigley up the street.' And she'd say 'Well, she has three tons of coal sitting out in front of her house. See that it gets put in.' I could hardly move, and I'd say, 'Ma, it's raining.' And she'd say, 'Yeah, it's raining. Go do it.' And I did."

My dad's disciplinary rules were not quite as stringent. Despite having allergies and asthma as a kid, I was responsible for mowing the fields on weekends prior to going out with friends. "Make sure you take an allergy pill and take your inhaler with you." If the fields didn't get mowed, I didn't get to go out.

My mom loved flowers and had many flower beds outside our house. In the spring it was my job, along with my younger brother Chad, to scatter the mulch in her gardens.

In the winter, I was responsible for feeding the cows and a horse named Moose. The horse was brought into his stall to eat, while the cows congregated under a shelter on the side of the barn. Hay bales were stored on the second floor of the barn, where sliding doors opened to reveal a trough below. I would open the doors, break up the bales of hay, and throw the hay down to the trough.

It was this type of discipline learned early on that helped me when I left home for college, and beyond. Once I began my stint in college, I was well versed in both studying and time management. The discipline that was taught to me by my dad paved the way for me to become a responsible human being.

In today's world we have "helicopter parents" who hover over their child's every move in an effort to protect them from pain, disappointment, and failure as they strive to achieve success. These parents need to focus less on coddling their children and more on teaching them the fundamentals of being accountable for their actions. Nowadays, so many parents want to be friends with their kids. It drives me crazy. Parents are supposed to be role models and provide discipline in their kids' lives so they can one day be positive contributors to society. Your job as a parent is not to prevent failure; it's to allow your child to fail, and teach them how failure can lead to future success.

The most successful people have failed countless times, but they have had the discipline to keep trying. If you're raising undisciplined kids, don't be surprised when they get passed over to be on the team or don't get hired for the job. Be more of a disciplinarian and less of a friend; your kids will appreciate it when they are older.

Life's Lesson #6

Don't Lie!

THE PARTY

There was one time in high school when my dad took discipline a step further, and that was when he caught me in a blatant lie. If there was one thing my dad would not tolerate, it was lying.

It was my junior year and there was a party at my friend Skip's house. His parents were gone for the week-end, so, of course, there were a lot of kids there. Needless to say, we proceeded to get plastered.

I wanted to spend the night at Skip's, but since his parents were gone, I knew my parents wouldn't allow me to stay. I got this brilliant idea to call my mom and have her speak with Skip's sister Missy, who would pretend to be their mom. My mom immediately saw through the ruse and told Missy to put me back on the phone. She told me that my dad would be there shortly to pick me up, and ended the call.

I was supposed to be waiting outside for him, but like an idiot, I was still at the party when my dad arrived.

He came into the house while we continued to drink in the basement. He had Skip and me come upstairs. My dad immediately began to question Skip as to where his parents were. I was standing behind my dad, trying to signal Skip on what to say, when my dad turned around and saw what I was doing. Without warning, he turned and slapped me across the face. Upon impact, the hat I was wearing flew across the room. He was really pissed!

When we got home, Dad woke up my brother Chad and made him come down to the kitchen where I was holding on to a chair to stay upright. I was still wobbling from the alcohol.

My dad, of course, made an example of me in front of my sibling.

"Look at your big brother—he can't even stand up! This is who you look up to. Stay away from the booze, and don't ever lie to me!"

The following morning, I woke up with a sore jaw, which I absolutely deserved. While most parents today would likely find a slap excessive, this wasn't the first incident involving underage drinking and lying. There were more reasonable conversations between father and son about my inappropriate actions long before this specific incident. Obviously, I was thickheaded, and the conversations were not getting through. A more "old-school" approach was needed in this situation, and it worked, because I never lied to him again.

Life's Lesson #7

Be a Good Teammate

FOOTBALL IS MY FAVORITE SPORT. INITIALLY THAT WAS because of Dad, but over the years the main reason was because of the teamwork that is needed to be successful. Eleven guys working together for the common goal of advancing the ball downfield, as far as possible, on each play. I also love it because of the life skills it teaches: sacrifice, patience, discipline, and focus, to name just a few. When I was eleven years old I didn't think about any of this.

My initial experience with organized football began in third grade at Calvert School. We practiced in full pads and were grouped by grade level (and accordingly, size), grades three and four on one team, and grades five and six on another. This way, no student would be physically outmatched by another. It was basically Football 101 in third and fourth grade. This is where I learned the basics of throwing, catching, blocking, and stances.

Everyone took turns at all positions, as well. At Calvert we ran the old single-wing formation. This offense does not utilize a designated quarterback, but rather four backs. The 2 and 4 backs typically line up behind the guards, while the 3 back (with the closest resemblance to a QB) lines up behind the center and usually receives a shotgun-style snap. The center can also snap the ball to the 2 or 4 back depending on the play call. The 1 back (or wing back) would line up outside the end on either side of the formation.

In fifth grade we got to play two games against Gilman, a K–12 college-prep school. I was so excited for my first-ever real football game, until just a few weeks before the game. The coaches told us the positions we would be playing, and mine was . . . center.

What the hell? Center? I wanted to throw the ball—be the QB, like Dad. You gotta be kidding me. Offensive line! Nobody wants to play offensive line.

I went home and told my dad the horrible news.

He sat me down and explained that first of all, center is a vital position, because without a good snap, most plays will likely fail. The second thing he talked about was being a good, coachable teammate: TEAM = Together Everyone Achieves More.

"You have to be coachable and do whatever is asked of you for the betterment of the team. Execute your assignment to the best of your ability on every play. When you do what coaches ask of you, other opportunities can arise," Dad said.

I couldn't really argue with him about this. He obviously knew what he was talking about.

Being the first game ever for both teams, it's not a shock to say the scoring was very limited. In fact, neither team had scored halfway through the fourth quarter. In addition to playing center, I was also the punter. I had plenty of action punting in this game. In the single wing we rarely, if ever, attempted a forward pass.

That was until the coach called for a fake punt. I was asked to throw the ball to our end. The play worked; we scored, and won the game. My first official TD pass. Being a good teammate had paid off.

ACADEMICS COME FIRST

My dad allowed me to play football for Calvert because it was so organized and carefully executed, making big hits and injuries a rare occurrence. I really wanted to play youth football, like Pop Warner, but my dad would not allow it. Each year I would ask him if I could play, and he would always reply with the same phrase: "Not until you get some hair down there."

Finally, eighth grade arrived (as did the hair—or should I say, peach fuzz). Either way, I was now old enough to play youth football!

My dad took me to the Lutherville-Timonium Recreation Council (LTRC) field to sign up to play. I was so excited! They gave me my uniform, helmet, and shoulder pads, and when I got home, I laid it all out on the floor of my room. I couldn't wait to start playing!

But my excitement at becoming a gridiron great would come to a screeching halt when I failed a test at school, the same week we were to start practice. With education first and foremost with my dad, he told me I wouldn't be playing football that year. I had to return all my equipment to the LTRC, and I also had to tell the coach *why* I wouldn't be playing: My after-school hours would be spent studying!

Lesson—or should I say, *lessons*—learned.

Life's Lesson #8

Winning Is All That Matters

BECAUSE CALVERT FOOTBALL WAS SO CAUTIOUSLY played, I was never really "popped" or hit hard until high school, when I experienced the pain of an excruciating hit to the solar plexus. In my freshman year at St. Paul's High School, I played corner on the varsity team. I was five-foot-ten and weighed a whopping 135 pounds. That season we played against Brooklyn Park. They had a powerful senior running back who was approximately six-two and weighed somewhere around 200 pounds.

I will never forget the one play where he plowed into the secondary on a sweep. At that point, I was the only thing between him and the goal line. I got down as low as I could, positioning myself to try and tackle him. Apparently, I wasn't low enough, as his knee hit me in the chest and knocked the wind completely out of me. It was a kind of pain I had never experienced before. I was in total agony and thought I was going to die. On a positive note, the enormous running back *did* fall to the ground, so I'll take credit for the tackle—although most likely, he tripped over me. Sometimes you just need a little luck.

Due to my minor impairment, I came out of the game for only a few plays before returning. In the end, we beat Brooklyn Park, and that's all that really mattered.

After my dad broke the passing record for touchdowns in consecutive games, he was asked how he felt. His response: "I never knew that I was throwing touchdown passes in every ball game and setting some kind of a record. Who knows . . . I don't look at the record books. Did we win? That's all I cared about."

My dad was always a fierce competitor, both on and off the field. It's one of the outstanding qualities he passed on to me.

THE WINDS OF CHANGE

Life's Lesson #9

Be 100 Percent Committed

I Want to Be a Football Player

My dad once said, "In school, I think it was either in the seventh or the eighth grade, we had a substitute teacher by the name of Mrs. O'Connor . . . beautiful lady . . . I had a bad crush on her. She went around the room and asked everybody what they wanted to do with their life, and when she got to me, for some reason—and don't ask me why, because I don't know—I said, 'I want to play professional football.'"

I shared my dad's aspirations to play pro football. I had it all figured out: My dream was to be the starting quarterback for the University of Miami and then be drafted into the NFL.

It wasn't long until I realized that I'd set the bar a bit high.

In 1991, when I was a junior in high school, I was interviewed by the *Baltimore Sun*. During the interview I mentioned that I wanted to play football for Miami. The story was picked up by the Associated Press, and remarkably, I soon received a recruitment letter and questionnaire from "The U." My dad and I decided to visit Miami and take in a game. Prior to the game, we visited the Miami locker room. It was there I met Gino Torretta, then Miami's starting quarterback, who would win the Heisman Trophy in 1992.

Although I'd grown a bit since my freshman year—I was now six-one and weighed 165 pounds—I could still turn sideways and hide behind telephone poles. Gino was a sophomore at Miami and was six-foot-two, weighing in at 215 pounds. All the players looked so big to me. It was at this moment I realized that pro football might not be part of my future. I'm sure my dad knew I was not cut out to be a professional football player, but he believed in following your dreams. He allowed me to come to the realization on my own.

Since the University of Miami was not going to be a realistic option, I applied to Louisville, Michigan State (for lacrosse), Ohio Wesleyan University (OWU), and Randolph Macon, located in Virginia. My goal was to play football and lacrosse in college. After recruiting visits to Randolph Macon and OWU, I chose to attend the latter, a small, private, liberal arts college located in Delaware, Ohio, just north of Columbus.

The reason I chose Ohio Wesleyan was because of Coach Leland Rogers. He came to St. Paul's to recruit me for lacrosse. At that time, St. Paul's was ranked number one in the country for high school lacrosse. When I explained to the coach that I wanted to play both lacrosse

Figure 2.1   After my final high school football game, in 1992.

and football, he said it wouldn't be a problem, as he was not only the head coach for lacrosse, but also an assistant coach for football.

OHIO WESLEYAN UNIVERSITY

The spring of my freshman year, I pledged to Alpha Tao Omega (ATO), along with eleven other students. A large percentage of the brothers were on the football team. Rush Week was in early spring, followed by Hell Week, which lived up to its name (and then some). We couldn't take showers and had to wear the same clothes all week. Two other pledges and I were on the lacrosse team, and even though we practiced every day, we still weren't allowed to shower.

One day one of our fraternity brothers took pity on us and allowed us to shower for one minute. We then got dressed, putting on the same clothing we'd had on before we took our showers. To add to this madness, we had to perform drinking games. One of those games had to do with relay-drinking and chugging Mad Dog 20/20.

For those of you who don't know, MD 20/20 is a fruit-flavored wine that comes in a 20-ounce bottle and contains 20 percent alcohol. It comes in a variety of flavors, but is still somewhat of a rotgut drink.

Four to five pledges lined up in three lines, each representing the first letter of the fraternity name (line A, line T, and line O). Thirty-gallon garbage cans were placed nearby, to be used for puking and peeing. The first pledge in each line was given a full bottle of Mad Dog. He would drink as much as he could, then pass it on to the guy behind him. The ritual would be repeated until the team that drank the required amount would be declared the winner.

While finishing off massive quantities of MD 20/20 probably wasn't what Dad had in mind when he taught me to be 100 percent committed, I chose not to make exceptions to lessons learned.

Life's Lesson #10

Support and Make Time for Your Children

Parents' Weekend and ATO Golf Tournament
Each year, Ohio Wesleyan hosted a parents' weekend. In the fall of my freshman year, both of my parents attended the festivities, including the football game. This meant a lot to me, because my parents were no longer able to attend my games on a regular basis. My brother Chad was now playing high school football, and Mom and Dad made it a point, as they had done with me, to support Chad.

In the spring, ATO also hosted a fathers' weekend, a great event that allowed dads and their sons to spend the entire weekend together. On Saturday there was a father-and-son golf tournament. My dad and I had an early tee time because I had a lacrosse game scheduled for the afternoon.

Following a weekend of fun and quality time with my dad, I heard many stories from my ATO brothers about how their dads thought it was so cool to "spend time with Johnny U." My dad, as always, was humble and genuine.

Figure 2.2   Family Weekend, Fall 1993, at OWU.

He never put on airs, and he despised those who used their celebrity status to do so. That weekend he was just another dad spending time with his son.

During spring break of that same year, my lacrosse team traveled to the Baltimore area to play a series of games. While we were there, my parents played host to our entire team and coaching staff at our farm in Maryland. I was so very fortunate to have parents who were so supportive of me.

Life's Lesson #11

Don't Quit

Having played lacrosse since the age of five, I had developed a sincere love for the sport, as well as respect for my teammates. These are the reasons why I was so excited to be given the opportunity to play college sports at Ohio Wesleyan. Unfortunately, my freshman lacrosse season at OWU turned out to be one I would rather forget.

It's an unwritten rule that freshman team members have to "pay their dues." It's expected that they will perform the grunt work, like carrying the equipment bag for the veteran players and moving goals. Back then, they also had to deal with hazing. In my case, they cut my hair to look like a Colts helmet. I actually found it funny and kept up the style for a couple of months.

What I didn't like was the verbal and, at times, physical harassment I received throughout the season from some of the upperclassmen on the team. It became so bad that I wanted to quit, but quitting was never an option. My dad always taught us to never quit—to finish what we started. I completed the season, but chose not to play lacrosse in my sophomore year.

When I had decided to attend OWU, my goal was to receive a degree in education and to coach both high school football and lacrosse. Outside of my parents, some of the most influential people in my life have been my teachers and coaches. Mr. Whiteley, Coach Broc, Mr. Tullai, Coach Collins, and Mr. Reuss were all incredible educators and coaches who helped mold me throughout my teenage years. I hoped to have the same impact on future student-athletes as well. The fact that I would have summers off was also a welcome incentive!

But upon completing my freshman year, I decided to change my career path to pursue a degree in sports business. From there, my ultimate goal was to become an NFL agent. In the spring of 1995, I contacted my high school college advisor and varsity lacrosse coach, Mr. Whiteley. I told him that I wanted to transfer from OWU to a university that offered a sports business major. At the time, schools that carried this major were few and far between. After researching them, Mr. Whiteley recommended that I apply to Elon University in North Carolina, Auburn University, and the University of South Carolina (USC). I applied to each, and to my surprise, was accepted by all three.

My favorite city on the East Coast has always been Charleston, South Carolina, a beautiful place with gracious Southern charm. I had the opportunity to spend some time with family friends on the Isle of Palms, just outside Charleston, and fell in love with the area. The USC campus is located in Columbia, just a few hours' drive from Charleston. I decided to become a Gamecock, and arrived on campus in August of 1995 without ever visiting the school. Something just told me this would be the right choice.

THE UNIVERSITY OF SOUTH CAROLINA—A NEW SCHOOL, A NEW BEGINNING

Upon my decision to transfer to South Carolina, I contacted the university's football office to find out when their two-a-day summer practices were set to begin. One of the assistant coaches answered the phone and told me to just come out when I arrived on campus. This sounded a little strange to me, but I decided it best to comply with his instructions.

A few days before classes started, I arrived on campus and moved into my new dorm. I was in a two-bedroom suite with three people I had never met. Looking back, I should have thought this through a little more, as sleeping in a dorm room with strangers was very uncomfortable for me. On top of it all, these roommates were not exactly welcoming. *So much for Southern hospitality.*

The following evening my dad and I arrived at Williams-Brice Stadium where football practice was being held. We walked over to the gate but found it locked. There was no one around to open it for us. Finally, we got the attention of Coach Shealy, the team's equipment manager. He walked over to the gate, and I introduced myself and my dad and told him I was there to meet with the coaches. The coach appeared to be a bit awestruck as he stood there face-to-face with "Johnny U."

"Hold on, I'll be right back!" he said. He took a moment to speak with the head coach, and they let us right in. Once on the field, my dad and I had the opportunity to watch the rest of practice. When it was over, the coach introduced my dad to the team and asked him to say a few words. Of course, he did.

Having grown some since my visit to the University of Miami's locker room, I realized the players didn't seem as intimidating as they had back then. Of course, many of the USC players were still massive in size, and their athleticism far surpassed mine; still, being a little older and wiser made me feel a lot more comfortable.

The first player to introduce himself to me was the senior starting quarterback, Steve Taneyhill. Steve was a Pennsylvania boy, like Dad, who hailed from the town of Altoona. Although Steve had some cockiness about him on the field, he was a good friend to me.

Life's Lesson #12

Working Hard Pays Off

PLAYING FOR THE GAMECOCKS

Due to transfer rules, I had to redshirt the 1995 season, although I was still allowed to practice. I was a decent Division III athlete, but nowhere close to a Division I football player. The speed and athleticism of the players at this level was something I had never experienced. To be honest, I felt I didn't even deserve to be on the team. But at the same time, my dad's words continued to push me. "Work hard and stick with it!" And I knew he was right.

I worked hard, was never late, and gave maximum effort in the weight room, at practice, and throughout the off-season. I earned the respect of my teammates and many of the coaches. All of my hard work finally came to fruition in my senior year. That final season I played on special teams units, and even got in a few snaps at quarterback.

But there was still one man whose respect I had yet to earn—my quarterback coach. This coach, who shall remain nameless, was an extremely talented college quarterback. He even played a few years in the NFL and USFL. Unfortunately, his career was compromised due to poor off-field decisions.

One day I was speaking to my dad about this coach and happened to mention him by name. My dad immediately recognized who he was and informed me of his somewhat shady past. I told my dad that the coach had changed his life for the better and found God.

"I didn't know God was lost!" was his quick response.

To say he was unimpressed would be an understatement.

Life's Lesson #13

Be Your Own Person and Be Judged as Such

AT LEAST GIVE ME THE CHANCE

When I was young, my dad instilled in me that I was my own person and should be judged as such. He also stressed that under no circumstances should *anyone* expect me to be him, or compare me to him. If they did, they should be considered "ignorant asses." Fortunately for me, this was never an issue growing up.

But things were about to change when I transferred to Carolina. My quarterback coach became that ignorant ass. Case in point: If I threw a bad pass in practice, it was not unusual for him to say, "Your dad wouldn't have thrown a ball like that."

I knew my athleticism and talent was far less than many of the other players on the team. Our starting quarterback, Anthony Wright—who would go on to play in the NFL and earn a Super Bowl ring with the New York Giants—was injured in the eighth game of the season against Tennessee. He was replaced by a *freshman* by the name of Vic Penn, bumping me into the backup role. Penn played the best he could, but Carolina was totally outmatched by the Volunteers. I never played a single down.

Our final game was against Clemson. It was also the final game of my college football career, and both my parents were in attendance.

Before I begin this story, you need to know that throughout all of my prior years as a player on many sports teams, my dad was always quiet. He had never once said a word to any of my coaches—that is, until now.

Clemson kicked our ass up and down the field that night in Columbia. At the start of the fourth quarter, Carolina was down, 40–14. The fact that it was Senior Night and the game all but over, I was hopeful that I might get a few snaps in at quarterback. However, even with a 26-point deficit, I never played a down.

On the field following the game, my dad and I were approached by the quarterback coach. He said to my dad, "Hey, John. Really sorry we couldn't get Joe in toward the end of the game. Just ran out of time." My dad responded with, "What was wrong with the start of the fourth when you were down almost thirty?" The coach, who didn't have much of a response, slithered away into the crowd.

My dad had experienced a similar situation with the Pittsburgh Steelers and could completely relate to my situation in the Clemson game. It was my dad's rookie season with the Pittsburgh Steelers, and one night during training camp there was a knock on his dorm-room door. One of the staff relayed a message: Head coach Walt

Figure 2.3   Mom and Dad at USC Senior Night, in 1997.

Figure 2.4   Senior Night at USC.

Kiesling wanted to see him, and to bring his playbook so he could turn it in.

When my dad arrived at Kiesling's office, he was told, "We just can't carry four quarterbacks. We're going to have to let you go."

My dad got hot under the collar and responded with, "You know, I wouldn't mind being released or being cut if I'd had an opportunity to play and screwed up very badly. But you never even gave me the damn opportunity to play."

Owner Art Rooney would later say that Pittsburgh made a big mistake by cutting my dad . . . and they were right.

Life's Lesson #14

Discipline and Structure Are Key Factors

USC Club Lacrosse Team

It always haunted me that I didn't play lacrosse in my sophomore year at OWU, so you can imagine how ecstatic I was to find out that South Carolina had a men's club lacrosse team.

USC was part of the SouthEastern Lacrosse Conference (SELC). We played against schools such as Clemson, Tennessee, Georgia Tech, Vanderbilt, Auburn, Elon, and Emory, also from the Southeast region. It was nearing the end of Christmas break, and I began packing my lacrosse gear with excitement and extreme anticipation for the upcoming season.

Before I continue, I need to clarify that I was actually practicing for two sports. With Carolina being a Division I football program, we had "spring ball." This was foreign to me, as I had never experienced spring football practices. Someone jokingly told me, "In the South we have two seasons—football season and spring football season!"

Football practice was over by 5:30 p.m. This gave me a chance to eat dinner and then hurry to lacrosse practice, which began at 7:00 and ended at 9:00 p.m. Games were usually played on Saturday afternoons, which worked out perfectly, as football practice was over by midmorning. We had a winning lacrosse season that year and entered the championship weekend as the number one seed.

The games were played at the Citadel in Charleston. We ended up winning the championship in my favorite city in South Carolina! Just getting to play again and compete against other passionate players was a joy that I had truly missed.

*   *   *

In sports, everyone wants to be a starter, but those who begin their playing careers at a young age learn quickly that there is always someone bigger, faster, and better. You give it your all and do the best you can with the hand you are dealt.

But with any sport, there must be discipline and structure. Discipline is the key factor that molds each individual athlete and gives them the structure they need to succeed. Even though I was in over my head as a football player at South Carolina, the discipline I learned and the work ethic it required to try and compete at the Division I level paid off significantly for me as I became an adult, and eventually, a husband and father.

Life's Lesson #15

Don't Dismiss Any Dream as Too Big

THE CROSBY AND GARY HUDSON—
AN UNEXPECTED OPPORTUNITY

In May 1998, after graduating from USC, I drove up to Winston-Salem, North Carolina, from Columbia, South Carolina, to spend a few days with my parents.

Dad was playing in the Crosby National Celebrity Golf Tournament. By a stroke (bad pun intended) of good luck, a few players had dropped out of the event, and I got to play with actors Gary Hudson and Stephen Root. It turned out that Gary had become friends with my folks, having met up over the past couple of years at the event. He and my mom hit it off because she was in Virginia Beach throughout her high school years, and Gary grew up in Newport News, Virginia. (I'm sure Gary's good looks didn't hurt either.) My dad liked Gary because he is a straight shooter and can tell a good story. They spent a lot of time together at the various events after they finished playing golf. It was a fun couple of days and nights, hanging out with my parents and Gary.

Little did I know this would be the start of a twenty-plus-year friendship between Gary and me.

Eastern Athletic Services (EAS)

Following the golf tournament, I moved back to Baltimore, where I began my practicum (similar to an internship, and the final requirement for my degree) at Eastern Athletic Services. EAS is a full-service sports representation and management company owned by Tony Agnone. Tony's office and my dad's office were in the same building.

I wanted to become an NFL agent, and working with Tony and the other agents would be my first step toward that goal. After I completed my practicum hours, Tony offered me a job. The long-term plan was for me to continue working for EAS during the day while attending law school in the evening, the path I had chosen to follow to fulfill my dream of becoming a certified NFL agent.

Runaway Bride—Another Twist of Fate

I grew up in Baldwin, Maryland, a small country town in northern Baltimore County. My dad had always wanted to have land, with a lot of animals, and that's what we had. My dad bought a twenty-acre farm with dogs, cats, rabbits, cows, goats, chickens, a horse named Moose, and a miniature donkey named Drambuie—after Mom's preferred after-dinner libation.

One November morning, my dad was driving through the countryside when he came upon some film production

Figure 2.5 The original GOAT with his new goats at the farm.

Figure 2.6   Family photo taken at the farmhouse in the late
1990s.

trucks that had stopped traffic on the quiet country road. This was not something the people of Baldwin were used to seeing. As my dad made his way to the person stopping traffic, he asked what was going on. That someone was Maryellen Aviano, who would soon become another key person in my life. Maryellen told him they were filming *Runaway Bride*, the movie that reunited Richard Gere and Julia Roberts and was directed by Garry Marshall. Gere and Roberts had previously appeared together in *Pretty Woman*.

Maryellen immediately recognized my dad and, in the few short moments in which they spoke, was able to get his phone number. It turned out that Garry was a huge sports fan, and his birthday was coming up on

Friday of that same week. The production staff had made it a tradition to always have a surprise for Garry when his birthday coincided with production. Maryellen asked my dad if he wouldn't mind coming back to the set on Friday. He agreed, and asked her to call him with the arrangements.

On Friday afternoon, Dad, Mom, Paige, and I (Chad was away at college) arrived on the film set. We met with Garry, who was totally shocked and very excited to meet my dad.

Dad not only signed a football for Garry but also threw him a pass, which was captured in a photo by the on-set photographer. We also had the opportunity to meet many of the other actors: Christopher Meloni, Rita

Figure 2.7   First time meeting Garry Marshall on the set of *Runaway Bride*.

Wilson, Joan Cusack, Héctor Elizondo, Richard Gere, and Julia Roberts. We ended up spending a few hours on the set and watched a few scenes being shot.

This was my first time on a movie set, and I immediately fell in love with the experience (a far cry from becoming an NFL agent). Seeing everything come together behind the scenes was very intriguing. The amount of people it took to make a film and the cohesiveness of working together as a team was awesome. In addition to the actors, we also met many members of Garry's trusted team, including Maryellen (extras casting coordinator), Ellen Schwartz (first assistant director), and Tommy Hines (personal assistant to Garry). My mom and Maryellen struck up an immediate friendship that day.

Prior to leaving the set, Garry made an offer for us to return as extras in later scenes of the film. We gladly accepted. Paige and I became background extras in a restaurant scene, while my mom appeared in one of the wedding scenes. For me, being on set the second time was just as exciting as the first. It reminded me of the plays we used to put on at Calvert School. I loved acting and learning lines; in fact, after college I'd thought about becoming an actor. However, growing up playing sports and deciding on a career in sports business had deterred me from ever pursuing an acting career.

Dad ended up with a speaking role in a brief scene with Richard Gere. He is seated on a sidewalk bench in the fictional town of Hale when Gere's character, Ike

Graham, gets hit by a little old lady while walking down the sidewalk. Ike asks my dad, "Did you see that?" To which Dad responds, "I've been hit harder." Unfortunately, the line ended up on the cutting-room floor. (Garry wrote my dad a note apologizing for not being able to keep the line in the film. Being the quiet and humble guy that he was, I'm sure my dad was fine with it.)

THANKSGIVING WITH THE PRODUCTION TEAM

The film crew took a break for the Thanksgiving holiday. When shooting on location, most of the crew is made up of local hires, so being apart from loved ones isn't an issue. But Garry, Maryellen, Tommy, and a few of Garry's closest staff were all from California, and unable to travel home for the holiday.

When my mom found out about this, she invited the remaining production staff to our home for Thanksgiving dinner. (I'm sure the "Thanksgiving dinner with Johnny U" story has been told many times over the years.) A few members of the production crew came to the house and we had a great holiday celebration. Two people in particular, Tommy and Maryellen, became friends of our family and very good friends to me.

At dinner, I asked Maryellen about her next project. She told me she was working on the film *Any Given Sunday*. It was a football film directed by Oliver Stone that was scheduled to begin shooting in the spring of 1999.

A Disability Claim for Dad

Once the holidays were over, I went back to work at EAS. My first job was to put together a disability claim for my dad to be submitted to the Bert Bell / Pete Rozelle NFL Player Retirement Plan.

After playing eighteen years in the NFL and receiving dozens of vicious hits to his right arm, my dad had lost a great deal of strength in his right hand. He was unable to hold a coffee cup or tie his shoes. When playing golf, he needed to use a large Velcro strap to keep his right hand gripped to the golf club. His long game really suffered, but he was still deadly when it came to chipping and putting. Amazingly, he was still able to sign a perfect autograph despite having to place the pen between his middle and ring fingers.

Unfortunately, his claim was denied. To be honest, we weren't expecting a decision in Dad's favor due to how the rules were constructed to benefit the NFL. It should be noted that Dad's claim was submitted in 1999. With everything that has come to light in the past twenty-plus years regarding the long-term effects of injuries to retired players, many of the rules have been rewritten, and the NFL is doing a much better job of taking care of their retirees today. A lot of these changes are due to the hard work put in by Tracy Perlman and her team at the league office. The NFL has really stepped up to show how important NFL alumni are to the league as a whole. It's just sad they didn't do it sooner, so my dad could have benefited from it.

Life's Lesson #16

One-on-One Time Is Important

ANY GIVEN SUNDAY

One evening in February, Maryellen called our home. I was surprised to hear her voice at the other end of the line. At that time, she had begun working on *Any Given Sunday* and was calling to speak with my dad. Once he'd hung up, I went to his office to hear what the call was all about. Oliver Stone was inviting some former players to make cameo appearances in the film, and Maryellen wanted to see if my dad would be interested.

Throughout his lifetime Dad starred in countless commercials, some TV shows (*Coach*, *The Simpsons*), and movies (*Gus*, *M*A*S*H*, *Runaway Bride*). His opinion of TV / film production / acting and mine are polar opposites. He once told me in regard to production, "All you do is hurry up and wait." Needless to say, he wasn't interested in appearing in *Any Given Sunday*. That is, until I told him that I really liked my experience on *Runaway Bride* and wanted to do *Any Given Sunday*. Maybe I *could* be an actor? I asked him to tell Maryellen he would do it, but only if I could be in the film with him.

A few days later we got a call back from Maryellen who said Oliver was excited to have Dad in the film, and that I would be allowed to join him.

We ended up traveling to Dallas, Texas, in May 1999. We spent five days shooting at the Cowboys' stadium in Irving. Dad was the head coach of the Dallas Knights, and I was the backup quarterback. We can be seen on the sidelines together in the final game of the movie.

Oliver's directions were very simple. He told us, "You guys know what happens on the sidelines. Just act and react normally to the situations." While I knew Dad wasn't excited about being in the film, it meant a lot to me that we got to spend those days together doing something I was developing an interest in.

While shooting in Dallas, we had the opportunity to meet many of the actors on the film, including Cameron Diaz, Jamie Foxx, Dennis Quaid, Matthew Modine, Lauren Holly, and of course, Al Pacino. Everyone was nice and excited to meet Dad, but there were a couple of people who stood out among the rest.

The first was Lauren Holly. She came over and introduced herself to us, then turned to me and said, "I understand you want to be an actor."

I'm not sure how she found out, but I replied, "I'm very interested, but I've never done anything. This is only the second time I've been on a set."

"And you already have lines in a movie. That's pretty good. You should do it. You'll be great!" Lauren said.

Obviously, Lauren didn't have to say any of that. More than twenty years later, I can still picture her and remember this quick conversation.

The second person to stand out was Lauren Shuler Donner, one of the film's producers. I'm not sure how we got to talking, but during our conversation I mentioned my interest in acting. Lauren, like my dad, was very direct and honest. She said that being an actor was extremely difficult and ultracompetitive. Actors are told *No* way more often than *Yes*. You need to have a thick skin, be able to accept rejection, and keep going. She also said that if I did decide to pursue acting, and to move to Los Angeles, I should contact her. She would try to help me if she could.

Life's Lesson #17

You Have to Let Go

CALIFORNIA DREAMIN'

Dad and I finished our parts in the movie in late April 1999 and returned home to Baltimore. Over the next month, I thought long and hard about acting and possibly moving to California. I weighed the pros and cons before making a decision.

The pros:

1. I had become friends with Tommy and Maryellen, who were both willing to help me.

2. I also had my new friend Gary Hudson, who I spoke with about the move. He was willing to help me find a place to live.

3. Because of my lines in *Any Given Sunday*, I was eligible to join the Screen Actors Guild.

4. I had never been to Los Angeles, and I was always up for a new experience. (A few years ago, I had

moved to Columbia, South Carolina, sight unseen, for college, and that had worked out.)

5. I would be very close to the beach, and the weather would be awesome.

6. I was still young and single.

The cons:

1. I was working at EAS and on the right path toward becoming an NFL agent.

2. I would be leaving Mom, Dad, Chad, and Paige.

3. I wouldn't be able to be there for family if anything bad ever happened.

4. I didn't have a job set up. How would I make money to support myself?

5. I had zero acting experience.

I spoke with my parents about this life-changing decision I was about to make, and they were nothing but supportive. Despite spending an absurd amount of money on me and my education, they were willing to support whatever decision I made. The one thing my dad did say was, "Joe, you've never acted or even taken an acting class."

My response was "Who cares? There are acting schools in LA. I'll learn!"

I guess I'd made my decision. Within one year I had graduated from college, started working toward a career goal, been on two movie sets, and decided to change my career path and move 3,000 miles from everyone and everything I had ever known and loved. The main reason I decided to go was that I didn't want to look back and say, *What if?*

Before I headed to California, my parents told me that if things didn't work out, I could come back home. They would always be there for me, and would support whatever decisions I made in my life.

It's a good thing our driveway was one-tenth of a mile long, and straight, as it was hard to see with all the tears streaming down my face.

THIRD QUARTER

HOLLYWOOD AND THE STARS

Life's Lesson #18

Believe in Yourself, Because If You Don't, No One Else Will

FRIENDS IN HIGH PLACES: THE ROAD TO LA

A few weeks before moving to California, I met a girl by the name of Anne, a friend of a friend from Baltimore. I was telling her about my plan to drive out to the West Coast, and she said she was interested in doing the same thing. She asked if she could accompany me cross-country, adding that she would chip in for gas. This sounded great; I would have a copilot, as well as company for what I figured to be a four-day drive.

Our first stop was in Columbus, Ohio, where we stayed with KD, one of my ATO frat brothers. The second night we stayed in Aspen, Colorado, with one of Anne's cousins. As we were getting ready to leave the following morning, Anne informed me that she had changed her mind about going to Los Angeles and would remain in Aspen. Ninety-eight percent of all starstruck wannabe actors don't make it in LA, but she didn't even make it *to* LA!

From Aspen, I drove to Las Vegas and stayed the night at the Golden Nugget. My mom's stepbrother happened to be a pit boss there, and was able to hook me up with a free room. I had never been to a casino before, much less gambled in one, but as they say, "When in Rome . . ."

I decided to play some blackjack. Having never played before, I was unaware that there are some general rules to the game regarding when to "hit" and when to "stay." When said rules are not followed, other players can become pissed off, even irate, because it impacts their potential winning hand. Let's just say I wasn't at the table for too long.

One thing Dad didn't teach me was how to gamble. In hindsight, this was a good thing. I've lived in Las Vegas for the past fifteen years, and other than placing a few parlay bets on NFL games, I don't gamble.

The following morning, I left Vegas and drove the final leg to Los Angeles. Once in LA, I met with Gary Hudson, who immediately proved to be a big help. With his girlfriend out of town for the week, Gary arranged for me to stay at her apartment. This gave me time to get settled and look for a place of my own.

Searching for a Room—and a Roommate

With Anne staying in Aspen, I was now minus a roommate. Fortunately, I had an alternate plan. Before I left Baltimore, I had heard that Amy, one of my closest childhood friends, was moving to LA for the summer prior to enrolling in nursing school. She had planned on rooming with Melanie, her sorority sister from Wake Forest, who was coming out from New Jersey to begin law school in the fall. The three of us talked it over on the phone and agreed that I would begin the search for a place for all of us to live.

When they arrived in LA the following week, we made our final decision, renting an apartment just up the street from Sony Studios. There was one problem, however: It was summer, when typically not a lot of TV or movie production is going on. Finding work as an extra would be challenging, to say the least.

DON KLOSTERMAN

As luck would have it, my dad had a very close friend by the name of Don Klosterman. Don was once the general manager of the Baltimore Colts before becoming GM of the Los Angeles Rams.

My dad contacted Don to see if he might be able to help me find work, and soon after, I met with Mr. Klosterman for lunch at the Bel-Air Country Club in Los Angeles. After lunch he introduced me to the golf pro as well as the caddy master. Turns out Mr. Klosterman had put in a special request for me to be a caddy at the club—not a bad summer job! I typically caddied five to six days a week, and always for Mr. Klosterman when he played, which was usually multiple times a week. I also had the opportunity to caddy for James Garner, Al Michaels, and Roger Staubach. Hearing those vintage stories from these gentlemen and the respect they had for my father was remarkable!

Tommy Hines, Maryellen, and Daisy Duke

Another person I connected with right away was Tommy Hines, Garry Marshall's assistant. I first met with Tommy at Garry's office in Toluca Lake. We caught up a bit and I got to say hello to Garry.

After a few more visits to see Tommy that summer, Garry asked me if I played softball. I told him it had been a while (four years) since the last time I played.

"That's okay," Garry said. "Ya played sports, you're tall 'n' strong—you'll do well. Tommy will give ya the details. See ya this weekend."

I soon found out that Garry had a coed softball team called the Falcons, named after Garry's Falcon Theatre, that played in Burbank on Sundays. I ended up playing on the team for close to seven years. (More on the benefits of softball with Garry later.)

As fall was quickly approaching, TV production began ramping up. After a few phone conversations during the summer, Maryellen and I reconnected in person. Maryellen is a longtime veteran in the world of show business. She started out as a stuntwoman in film and television before moving on to become the extras casting coordinator on numerous feature films.

One of Maryellen's early stunt jobs was on *The Dukes of Hazzard*. It was here that she doubled for Catherine Bach, who played Daisy Duke. (Side note: When I was a young boy, I watched *The Dukes of Hazzard* and *The Incredible Hulk* every Friday night. It's safe to say that along with millions of other boys, Daisy was my very first Hollywood crush.)

Maryellen asked me to meet her at Central Casting in Burbank. She helped me sign up to become an extra/background actor. She then escorted me around the office and introduced me to many of the casting managers she had worked with over the years. She asked them to keep me in mind when extras were needed for TV shows and movies they were working on.

For the next two and a half years I worked basically five days a week on various sets, acquiring a hands-on education in TV and film production. Observing actors as they worked and studying the multifaceted roles of the crew was an incredible learning experience for me. Good thing Dad stopped his car that day in Baltimore and asked what was going on!

GARRY MARSHALL—MY BOSS, MY TEAMMATE, MY FRIEND

A Hollywood icon, Garry Marshall enjoyed a career that spanned more than sixty years. He began as a writer, but over time branched out into acting, directing, and producing. Most people remember Garry for his creation of classic TV shows such *as Happy Days*, *Laverne & Shirley*, and *Mork & Mindy*. He was also widely known for directing movies that grossed well over $100 million at the box office—*Pretty Woman*, *Runaway Bride*, *The Princess*

Diaries, The Princess Diaries 2, Valentine's Day, and New Year's Eve.

I remember him for his friendship and loyalty to all the FOGs (Friends of Garry). If you were a FOG, which I was honored to be, Garry would routinely find ways to have you in his films. Like many other young people in Garry's circle, I became a FOG by playing on the Falcons softball team.

Garry was our pitcher and oldest teammate. Most of the players on the coed team ranged in age from their early twenties to late thirties, and had ties to Garry through the entertainment industry. We played Sundays on various fields throughout Burbank. Although I was initially hesitant about playing, due to my lack of experience, being a part of this team is one of my fondest memories from my years in LA. The teammates were great, most were good athletes, and we won a few league championships over the years. I won't hesitate to say that Garry probably liked winning those championships more than he did receiving some of his industry awards.

The Princess Diaries was shot in 2000 and released in 2001. It was filmed in Los Angeles and San Francisco. I was primarily a stand-in on this film, but Garry was nice enough to give me a role as "Coach Joe Ewe." (Nice play on words, Mr. Marshall!) I worked every day of production in both LA and San Francisco and learned a great deal by observing the actors—mainly Héctor Elizondo, Julie Andrews, and a young soon-to-be star, Anne Hathaway.

In 2004, I was fortunate enough to work on the film *Raising Helen*, starring Kate Hudson and John Corbett. I played the role of "Hockey Announcer."

Garry Marshall was an incredible man. With all of his talent and success, he could easily have been arrogant and self-absorbed. Fortunately for me and many others, he wasn't. Instead, he was one of the most humble, genuine, and generous people I have ever had the pleasure to meet, and to work for. He reminded me a lot of my dad in that way—just a lot funnier!

Figure 3.1   With Garry Marshall on the set of *Raising Helen*.

Playhouse West: Mr. Robert Carnegie

Although the years I spent as a background actor on TV and movie sets proved to be extremely beneficial in my early development in production, I still wasn't *really* acting. You can only learn so much by observing. You have to actually *do* the work to improve your craft.

In the spring of 2002, I went back to North Carolina for the Crosby golf tournament. Once again, I got to play with my now good friend, Gary Hudson. It was at one of the dinners that I met a fellow young actor named Burgess Jenkins. (Burgess is from North Carolina and most recently appeared in *Remember the Titans*, playing the role of Ray Budds.) As we continued our conversation, I asked him if he could recommend any acting classes in Los Angeles, and he told me he was currently studying at Playhouse West.

Playhouse West is owned by Robert Carnegie and cofounded with actor Jeff Goldblum. Robert was a past student of the legendary acting teacher Sanford Meisner, for whom the Meisner Technique of acting is named. I thanked Burgess for the information and his contact info and decided to check out the prestigious acting school when I got back to LA.

To be considered for acceptance, one must attend, watch, and observe a three-hour beginner class. Once class had concluded, you would then meet with Robert Carnegie. I did exactly that. While this next part might sound like bullshit, I promise you, it's all true.

After class was over, I sat down with Mr. Carnegie and introduced myself. Immediately he took notice of my last name and asked if I was related to John Unitas. When I affirmed that he was my dad, a huge smile came over Mr. Carnegie's face, and he let out a glorious laugh. He then proceeded to tell me the following story.

"I'm originally from Virginia and I grew up idolizing your father. In my area we could watch the Redskins with a crisp, clean picture, or the Colts in what looked like a snowstorm, with the occasional rolling of the screen. [If you are younger than forty-five, you will need to ask a parent what this means.]

"I always watched the Colts game because of your dad. He wasn't my favorite player because he was so good. I liked him because of his leadership qualities, the command he had of the offense, and the way his teammates responded to him. I would not only watch the games—I would study your father. I would read anything I could get my hands on about him. He was an amazing study of work ethic, attention to detail, and his character as a man. Oh my gosh, his character. None of today's professional players can come close to touching the character of your father."

Mr. Carnegie continued: "I saw your dad interviewed a couple of years ago, and he mentioned he had a son who had moved to LA to pursue an acting career. I wrote him a letter to tell him how much I looked up to him and how I tried to pattern myself after him. I also said that it would be my honor to have his son here at Playhouse

West. I didn't have your dad's address, so I just sent the letter to John Unitas, Baltimore, Maryland. I was hopeful that someone at the post office would know how to get it to him. Unfortunately, the letter came back. But now here you are. Life has a funny way of working out."

Mr. Carnegie not only accepted me into Playhouse West, but he also put me in his class—the same class with Burgess and many other new actors. For the next three and a half years I remained a loyal student of Mr. Carnegie's at Playhouse West. He taught me everything there is to know about acting. PHW is not for everyone. Back then, classes met twice a week, three hours at a time. Each month there was required reading to complete, as well as written book reports.

Upon successfully completing the beginner class, you moved on to scene study. This created more time to devote to learning lines and practicing with your scene partners outside of regular class hours. It's easy to say you want to be an actor, but putting in the actual work to *become* one is an entirely different thing. I absolutely loved it! In comparison, it's no different than practicing all week for the next game.

Whether it was acting or team sports, discipline was exactly what was required for me to become a good actor. Thankfully, I had learned all about this early on from Dad, and from playing sports. The competition in Hollywood is fierce, not to mention vicious. You must discipline yourself to work *every day*. If you don't, there are others who will, and they will have a better chance at getting the next job.

During my years at Playhouse West, I learned how to act, and how to study scenes and scripts. I had a small role in a play called *Welcome Home, Soldier* which ran at PHW for twenty-five years, beginning in 1991. The play was supportive of Vietnam veterans and explored how society responded to vets returning home from the war. (A thank-you to all the brave US military men and women, for your service to our country during the Vietnam War!)

My favorite play was one in which I was a co-lead, called *Lone Star*, by James McLure.

This one-act comedic play is about two Texas brothers, Roy and Ray (I played younger brother Ray). Roy has recently returned from a hitch in Vietnam and quickly learns that the hometown he left was not the same he had returned to. The excitement and energy of live acting, along with immediate reaction from the audience (in this case, laughter), is quite intoxicating. I love making people laugh.

Mr. Carnegie was more than just my teacher. He became a mentor and close friend. He continued to correspond with my dad through letters, although, sadly, he never had the opportunity to meet my dad in person.

The following is correspondence between Mr. Carnegie and my dad:

May 1, 2002
Dear Mr. Unitas,

I can't thank you enough for the wonderful, autographed picture you sent me through your son, Joe.
My wife immediately went out to get it framed in a
special way, and it will be placed on the wall in my
favorite area of our house. I just talked to my father
yesterday on the phone and told him about it, and he
was as excited as I was. I was always active in sports
as a kid, and was a big fan of football and baseball,
and knew all the players. But I can honestly tell you
that there is not a single athlete I would rather have
an autographed picture from than yourself. You're in
a class by yourself. I really appreciate so much you
doing that for me.

I don't know if Joe told you the story I told him.
It was maybe a year or less ago that I was flipping
through the channels, and there you were on a home
shopping show. I immediately turned on the recorder,
and still have the show. Your wife called and talked to
you during the show. And you mentioned that your
son was in L.A. and wanted to be an actor. I wrote
you a letter, but not having your address, I just mailed
it to general delivery, Baltimore, Maryland. It came
back undelivered. I told you in the letter how much
I had learned from you when I was a kid, and how I
studied you and your approach to playing football for
years. I mentioned this because you had been such an
inspiration to me and meant so much to my family
growing up.

I also mentioned that I run a top-notch acting school. Over the years, I have worked with some incredible actors, including Michelle Pfeiffer, Ashley Judd, Jim Carrey, Jeff Goldblum (who teaches at my school), and recent Golden Globe winner James Franco, who won for the James Dean movie that I worked on with him for months. He will be seen in the next "Spider Man."

Even though you never got my letter, a few months later this young fellow interviewed with me and said his name was Joe Unitas. I could tell just from looking at him who he was, but I asked, "Are you John's son?" He said he was. I then told him the story about the letter I had written you. It turned out the film director Garry Marshall had recommended my school. Garry, like most in Hollywood, knows of our excellent reputation, and he even participated in our film festival last year. Joe had liked what he had seen of the class he sat in on and wanted to take the class. Even though the letter came back undelivered, I still told him I had made an agreement with his dad that if he were to come to my school, there would be no charge. And so, he started a couple of weeks later.

I think that's some story, and I am very happy to have Joe in class. I put him in the best class in the school and have done some special things for him since. I will continue to do everything I can to help him, and I will keep track of opportunities for him. He has been raised well. He's very polite and responsible, and very good-natured, with a great sense of humor.

He takes his work seriously and he is making excellent progress.

As a matter of fact, he is so well-adjusted and balanced, one wonders what he is doing in this crazy profession populated by so many neurotics. If you ever have a concern for him or want to ask anything about how he is doing, feel free to write or call. I also told Joe that if you are ever out here, I live on a golf course, and we could all play a round. There was a time I had a place in Rancho Mirage and Deacon Jones was living there one year—this is about six or seven years ago. I got to know him and would play golf with him. I asked him about you, and he said you were the quarterback he most respected.

One of the things I told you in the letter was how we would watch you on TV in the 1950s and early '60s. We lived in Berryville, Virginia, about 60 miles south of D.C., so we got the Redskins games on the local channel fine. But your games were on a Baltimore station that was hard to pick up, and so it often looked like every game was played in the snow because of the poor reception. But we always watched the Colts games and were loyal Colts fans. We would rather watch you and your team with terrible reception than watch any other team with a clear picture. I thought that made the point about what Johnny Unitas meant to football and the times.

We were not well off financially, but we did get to see you play once. My father got tickets to a Redskins game when you were playing them, and we arrived hours early to make sure we did not miss a minute of the warm-ups. I can still see number 19—it was the blue uniform—to this day. And number 82—Raymond Berry, after whom I patterned myself, as I was an end. It is funny the things that have meaning to kids and help them grow up and be interested in things. I do not think kids have now what we used to have.

Now I don't watch football, except for the Super Bowl. I really stopped following it when you stopped playing. I always tell my students to study the actors of the '50s, like Brando, Dean, Clift, and McQueen, because they were the best. But kids can't do that with sports. I grew up watching the game at its highest level and quarterbacked at its highest level. There is nothing to watch in comparison. And to make matters worse, the absurd celebrations after every play, and the overall lack of good sportsmanship, completely turns me off.

Back in the mid-1980s Joe Namath's wife came to my classes. She brought him one day to a special school event. I talked to him for a while and told him how bad I felt when the Jets beat the Colts in Super Bowl III. He told me he did not feel bad about it. Out of politeness, I never told him what I and an awful lot of folks believe—that if you had been put into that game at the beginning of the second half—injury or no injury—the Colts would have won.

So, I have gone on to thank you for more than just the picture. How can you thank someone for being a part of the fabric of your growing up and development—for you being a role model to me, when athletes really were role models.

Joe lent me great book about the Colts, *When the Colts Belonged to Baltimore*. There were many wonderful stories in there about you, many of which I knew because I have read so much about you. But my favorite story was the one where your friend, Romeo, I think was his name, wanted you to sign a football for a kid in the hospital. You took the ball to the hospital yourself.

I know you have had a tough life in so many respects, and I have felt bad about that. But I'm a religious man, and I am confident that the character you have built, and your decency, will see a just recompense of reward someday. In the meantime, don't ever doubt there are hordes of grown-up kids like me out there who will never stop appreciating, and will never forget, number 19.

With sincere thanks,
Robert Carnegie

*   *   *

June 23, 2002
Dear Mr. Carnegie,

I can't thank you enough for your wonderful letter from May 1 concerning my son Joseph. First of all, please accept my apology for being so long in answering your letter. I certainly appreciate what you are doing for him. He is a very hard worker, and he won't disappoint you. When he told me he was going to California to become an actor, I thought he was out of his mind. I said, "Joe, first of all, you should have some acting ability, and to the best of my knowledge, you haven't even attended a drama class." Joseph has always been pretty determined. Once he makes his mind up, you might as well get out of his way.

His mother and I are very proud of him, as well as our other two children. I don't know if Joe has mentioned to you that he is going to get married in September, and of course the family will be coming out to California for the wedding. If your schedule is not too tight, we could get together. That certainly was a great story about how you and Joe got together. It's nice to hear that my life has had some positive effect on people.

The game of football has changed somewhat over the past years. It's still blocking and tackling, but the people doing it can be hard to take. Not to mention that 29 percent are felons.

Well, I guess I have been rattling on enough. Again, thank you for looking out for Joe. I am looking forward to meeting you in a few months.

Thanks again,
John Unitas

*   *   *

July 17, 2002
Dear Mr. Unitas,

I very much appreciate hearing from you. Your letter was a lot of fun to read and filled with the kind of common sense and good humor I remember from all your interviews. Thank you very much!

I'll give you a little update on Joe. I have to tell you I shared your concern about his relative lack of previous interest in acting. Most actors are drawn to the craft at a fairly early age, but not everyone. Many do not get interested in acting until college, or even later. One of my friends, Rod Steiger, who sadly just passed away, was a great actor, and he came to it quite late. He had served in the Merchant Marines and fought in World War II. After the war he was work-ing in an accounting position, or something like that, and he noticed all the girls were missing on Thursday nights. He found out they went to an acting class, so he decided to go, to be around the girls. It was there that he found out he had an aptitude for the craft and took classes that were paid for by his GI Bill. He went on to win an Academy Award for Best Actor some years later. So, there are some good exceptions to the rule.

As to his progress in class, he has worked hard, as you said he would. He is a very dedicated and serious student. He caught on to what we teach very quickly, which is a good sign. Some labor forever to try and figure out how to do what we teach. But such was not the case at all with Joe. He's done so well that one of the older actors in the class, who has done lots of film and TV work, said that he was using Joe as his example for how to do this. I thought it was quite a compliment. And indeed, Joe is a fine example of how to do the work we teach. I have to say very little to him. In my style of teaching, I try to say very little anyway. Joe makes it easy.

So, while this is a very good sign, there is much to do yet. First we teach the fundamentals of acting through exercises. Kind of like sports, one first has to learn the basics. After the basics are learned and one starts to play the game, then the degree of talent or ability starts to show itself. In sports, that talent or ability, if substantial enough and combined with other elements, can lead to real opportunity. In acting, it is actually more difficult. Besides acting ability, there is the element of a person's basic look and personality, which is a big factor. Those with the edge in that department can get many more opportunities than others who have more talent or ability. But again, using Steiger as an example, he never had that edge but still rose to great prominence.

There is an 85 to 90 percent unemployment rate among actors. Makes the Depression look like good times. It is easily one of the toughest professions on Earth to succeed in, let alone make a living. But if a person loves the profession, for whatever crazy reason, they are happier trying to do it than not. I have already talked to Joe about these realities and mentioned to him that he should be looking at the entire profession, not just acting. There is directing, producing, and so many other aspects to the business for those who love it. One of my students, Scott Caan (James Caan's son), although having starred in films and making a good living as an actor, has just finished directing his first film. He says he may enjoy that more than acting. So, you never know.

I have put Joe into his first play. I have enclosed a recent review. It's called *Welcome Home, Soldier*. It's been running for twelve years here at Playhouse West. It is in defense of the Vietnam veterans and an exposé of the so-called peace movement. It is the longest-running play in L.A. Joe will be in it the first Saturday of August. I did the same thing for Ashley Judd after I met her mother, as well as for James Franco. Normally I never put beginning students in plays. I've made those two exceptions in the past, so Joe is in good company. He'll work with our advanced students, and he'll get to appear in many scenes. He won't have any written lines, but neither did Ashley. He will get to say things and be part of the action for several hours. It will be a great experience for him. He'll appear in it the first Saturday of almost every month. That should help him a great deal.

I also arranged for Joe to be on the set with film star Jeff Goldblum. Jeff is close to starting a new TV movie, and I asked him if he would help Joe out by letting him watch him work and meet some of the other actors in the film. Joe has already spoken with Jeff and that is set to happen.

One other thing I've set up for Joe is his attendance at our film festival which takes place next weekend. Seating is limited, but I've made arrangements for him and his fiancée to be able to attend all three days. He'll learn a lot about all aspects of the business, and he'll see some of the films our students have produced over the past year.

So, I'm doing what I can, and it is a real privilege to try and give something back to the Unitas family. Joe did tell me about his upcoming marriage. He also told me that you might be coming early and would like to attend a class. Should that work out, my wife Maxine and I would love to take all of you to dinner. There is a very nice place not far from where we live, which isn't too far from the school. Needless to say, if there is any possibility of meeting you in person, or making your time out here more enjoyable, we would love to do so.

I hope everything is well for you personally and professionally. Thanks again for all the great memories.

Respectfully,
Bob Carnegie

I was set to be married on September 28, 2002. We had planned for my family to come out to California a few days prior to the wedding. Mr. Carnegie had offered to host my dad, Chad, and I for golf and lunch at his country club. But on September 11, 2002, my dad suffered a fatal heart attack at the gym and passed away at the age of sixty-nine. This was, without a doubt, the most traumatic event of my life. Fortunately, I had the support of my fiancée, my family, and even Mr. Carnegie to help me through this emotional time.

In seventeen days, I went from the emotional low of losing my father to the high of marrying my incredible wife, Dianna. Despite being years removed from PHW, I remain in contact with Mr. Carnegie to this day. He will forever remain a special person in my life.

ADULTHOOD: LOVE, MARRIAGE, FAMILY, AND RESPONSIBILITY

DIANNA

Baltimore is known by many who live there as *Smaltimore*. Although this city houses close to 600,000 people, with another 25,000 in surrounding Baltimore County, it seems like there are only a couple degrees of separation from knowing the stranger next to you. Some might find this annoying, but I feel it is one of the things that make being a native of Baltimore special.

After living in California for one year, I joined the Hollywood Men's Lacrosse Club. I quickly found this to be a bond found on both the East and West Coasts. I met other guys on the team from Baltimore who I knew of, through other friends, but never really got to know personally. Over the next three years we would play together on both Team Lax World and then Adrenaline. Most of the games were played in Los Angeles, Orange, and San

Diego Counties. The weekend road trips with the fellas—playing lacrosse, as well as doing some heavy partying after each game—was a lot of fun. To quote a line from a country music song, "We made a lot of memories I can't remember and some I'll never forget."

One of those unforgettable memories came in April 2001. The team was sponsored by Margaritaville, a bar in Newport Beach. One night, after one of our games, we decided to go there to eat and drink. Little did I know that Margaritaville was about to change my life forever.

Digger, one of the players on the team, lived on the Balboa Peninsula and had become good friends with one of his female neighbors, Daphne. He invited her to our game and then to the bar afterward. Not wanting to be the only girl, Daphne called her friend who worked at Fashion Island, a shopping mall nearby, and asked her to stop at the bar on her way home from work. Her friend's name was Dianna. We were all introduced, and everyone began talking.

Dianna was the most beautiful woman I had ever seen in person. One of the guys asked her if she knew who John Unitas was. She said no. He then proceeded to tell her he was a famous football player, and I was his son. She was not impressed by this at all, which I actually found refreshing.

Dianna and I spent a lot of time talking and laughing that evening. I have always believed that if you can make a woman laugh, you have a chance. I know this is true because there was no way she was impressed by my appearance. We had just played a lacrosse game, and I, like the rest of the team, had not had a chance to shower. I was wearing a T-shirt which I'd found balled up in the back of a teammate's truck, blue jeans so ripped any grunge band member would have been proud to wear them, and flip-flops held together with duct tape.

Earlier that day I had left my truck in Manhattan Beach and driven to Newport with some of my teammates. When it was time to leave the bar, the guys told Daphne they would take her home, which left me without a ride. Daphne volunteered Dianna to give me a ride back. "I can't take him to Manhattan Beach," Dianna replied. "My mom is at home with Clark."

Dianna *did* end up giving me a ride to Manhattan Beach after a pit stop at her home in Long Beach. On the way, she told me that Clark was her four-year-old son, and that she had been divorced since he was an infant.

I don't know what kind of response she was expecting, but I wasn't fazed at all. I believe I said something like, "Cool. I love kids. My dad had a total of eight children, so there were always young nieces and nephews around."

We arrived at her house around ten p.m. I waited in the car while she went in and asked her mom to stay longer, so she could drive me to Manhattan Beach. That must have been a fun conversation! Anyway, I met her mom before we left. This was definitely a record for me—meeting the mom within the first six hours of meeting her daughter. Her mom called Dianna multiple times as we drove to Manhattan Beach (probably to make sure she was still alive).

My mind wandered a bit during the drive as I tried to sort out what had just transpired. After Dianna dropped me off, I realized I hadn't even thanked her properly for taking me to Manhattan Beach to get my truck. I immediately called her and apologized for coming off as an ungrateful asshole. She laughed and brushed it off. Over the next week, we talked to each other on the phone more than I had ever talked to anyone.

It was during one of our extended conversations that I learned more about her. Dianna was born in Long Beach, California, the youngest of five children (she had three brothers and one sister). Her mom was from England and her dad from Jerusalem (Palestine).

The following week we went out with friends, and did the same the next week. At this point, the only time we'd been alone together was on our drive to Manhattan Beach. Finally, during the third week, Dianna drove up to Studio City, where I was living with three roommates. Since this would be our first real time alone, I wanted to take her to a special place.

One of my favorite spots in Malibu is a little beach called El Matador. To get there you have to park in a small lot that is just off the Pacific Coast Highway. Then you descend a very steep set of steps that go from the edge of the rock cliff down to the sand. Once on the beach, if you go north, there is a large rock that juts out into the ocean. If the tide is low you can go around the rock to a very secluded part of the beach. We spent the next hour there, enjoying the sunset before going to dinner.

Although Dianna and I had spent many hours talking in recent weeks, on this particular evening she was noticeably quiet and reserved. When I asked her what was wrong, she seemed nervous, and was hesitant to answer.

I'm not sure where it came from, but I said, "There's another guy, isn't there?"

She was shocked by my directness and that I'd figured out what the problem was. She said yes. To say I was also taken aback is an understatement.

Regardless of how I felt, I tried to play it as cool as possible. Even though there is no exact lesson that I'd learned from Dad for this situation, I chalked it up to sharing some of his traits. I remained calm and confident in what was, in reality, a very uncomfortable situation for both of us. I told her that I appreciated her telling me, but if we were going to continue to see one another, she would have to break things off with the other guy. I told her she could have a week to take care of the matter.

To her credit, she did what I asked, and from there our relationship took off. Within a few months I had moved to Long Beach, and by January 2002, we were engaged, setting the wedding date for September 28, 2002.

Life's Lesson #19

There Is Nothing More Important than Family

THE NFL NATION MOURNS A HERO

On the one-year anniversary of the 9/11 terrorist attack, I met Dianna for lunch at Fashion Island in Newport Beach, after which she returned to work.

As I was pulling out of the Fashion Island parking lot, I received a call from my mom. She was crying. She told me that my dad had had a heart attack at his workout facility and had passed away. This was the worst news I had ever received in my life. It was difficult for me to wrap my mind around it. Being so far away from my family at this horrific time frightened me.

I told my mom I had to tell Dianna, and then I would get on the earliest flight back to Baltimore. I was able to find Dianna and tell her the devastating news. She immediately told her manager what had happened, and we left together.

As soon as we arrived home, I got on the computer and booked two tickets on a red-eye flight that night. We packed our bags and spent the rest of the day crying and grieving, receiving many calls from loved ones and close friends. My dad's death had become national news.

Dianna and I landed in Baltimore early the next morning. My mom picked us up and we immediately drove to St. Joseph's Hospital, where I was able to view my dad's body. It was heartbreaking, but having my mom and Dianna there to support me was extremely helpful.

Upon leaving the hospital, we drove to my parents' home. Being the eldest of my siblings, I knew it was my responsibility to step up and take on a leadership role in planning my dad's funeral, reception, and anything else that was needed. That day and the next were spent answering calls and planning the family viewing, the funeral service at the Cathedral of Mary Our Queen, the transportation for the entire family, and the funeral reception.

Arrangements were made not just for my family and friends. My dad had been married before he and my mom married. That marriage produced five children. Their age range spans over eight years. The youngest sibling is eleven years older than me. Unfortunately, 2002 was not a good year for them. Their mother, Dorothy, had passed away just a few months prior to my dad's death.

The relationship between Dad's older kids and my family has always been cordial at best. I don't think I had spoken with any of them during the time I was in California, so it didn't feel right to reach out to them for help. Plus, they had their own families and children to take care of during this difficult time. Other than running into Kenneth, the youngest son from the first marriage, at a hospital in 2007, I have not seen or spoken to any of them since Dad's funeral.

DOROTHY JEAN HOELLE UNITAS

Dorothy and my dad were high school sweethearts who married after Dad finished college in Louisville. All the stories I have heard from family and their high school classmates depict Dorothy and Dad as polar opposites. Dorothy was very outgoing and boisterous and loved attention while Dad was reserved, a man of few words.

Dorothy had dreams of becoming a famous actress in Hollywood or on the New York stage, while Dad dreamed of becoming a professional football player. Unlike Dorothy, fame and fortune were not something my dad craved; in fact, he actually downplayed his own celebrity. When the Colts won the 1958 Championship Game, he was invited to appear on *The Ed Sullivan Show* in New York City. My dad graciously declined the invite and sent Alan Ameche, who scored the winning touchdown, to represent Baltimore.

In 1955, Dad and Dorothy welcomed their first child, a daughter, who they named Janice. At that time, Dad was just a guy playing sandlot football in Pittsburgh, Pennsylvania. Little did anyone know that in three short years, the future legendary Johnny U would be introduced to the rest of the nation in Yankee Stadium—a different New York stage than what Dorothy had envisioned as a young girl.

On December 28, 1958, the Baltimore Colts defeated the New York (Football) Giants in the first-ever sudden-death NFL Championship Game. Many consider this title game "the greatest game ever played." Whether this is true or not is up for debate, but there is no doubt it was the cornerstone upon which the modern-day NFL was built. By that time Dad and Dorothy had two children, Janice and John Jr.

The era of the 1950s was obviously quite different from today. Women were expected to stay at home, raise a family, and care for the house while the men went out and worked to provide financial support for the family. It's my opinion that Dorothy's dream of becoming a famous actress was terminated on December 28, 1958.

Over the next few years, three more sons were born—Robert, Christopher, and, finally, Kenneth, in 1965. Having a wife and five children to support meant that Dad could not be home as much as he would have liked. The NFL contracts were not the lucrative ones of today. In my dad's rookie season, he signed for $7,000. He and most of his teammates had to work a second job in order to make ends meet. He worked a regular job in the morning and went to practice in the afternoon.

I believe that over the years, the time he spent away from home and family created resentment in Dorothy and tension in their marriage. He was the famous one, living the life that Dorothy had only dreamt of. I have heard many stories over the years from family members and teammates alike about Dorothy's public outbursts and flat-out rudeness to fans, especially women, when she was out with my dad. This caused him a great deal of embarrassment and grief. They separated and finally divorced in 1973, prior to Dad's last season as a professional football player.

Witnessing their father's subsequent marriage to my mom was likely hard for his children to accept. Having a second family, which included three more children—me in 1974, Chad in 1978, and Paige in 1982—most likely fanned the flames of resentment for Dorothy. She never remarried, and kept the Unitas name till the day she died.

Now that Dad was retired and considered the greatest quarterback of all time, he had much more time to

Figure 4.1   We visited Dad and Brent Musburger on *The NFL Today* set at CBS during Wild Card Weekend in 1985.

spend with his second wife and three younger children. As mentioned, he tried his best to never miss a game, a play, or a music recital that my younger siblings or I participated in.

I give my mom a lot of credit. She always included the five older kids in holidays and birthday celebrations. Chad and Christopher (Dad's third son) actually share December 18 as their birthday. For many years we had dual birthday parties that all eight of the children attended, along with their spouses and grandchildren. Accolades to most of the older five, as well, for taking on a difficult situation and making the most of it when we were all together.

As a child and throughout college, the majority of my memories with them were positive. But sadly, this all came to an abrupt end when Dad passed away.

Life's Lesson #20

Be a Leader and Not a Follower

THE FUNERAL

Tuesday, September 17, 2002, was the day of Dad's funeral. I had trouble sleeping the night before due to the incredible number of things running through my mind. Did I forget anything about the transportation? Did I pay all the vendors for the reception? Would everyone arrive at my parents' home early enough to be at the church on time?

Early Tuesday morning, I went downstairs to get something to eat and turned on the local news station which was broadcasting the morning wake-up show. A reporter was giving a live report from outside the cathedral, talking about traffic concerns around the church that could impact people getting to work. In the background I saw one of Chad's friends, as well as many others, already at the site. This was at least three hours before the memorial service was scheduled to begin!

Everyone, including older siblings, nieces and nephews, and our closest family friends, made it to my parents'

Figure 4.2 Photo of Dad from his funeral program.

home on time. From the number of limos, police, and commotion outside of the house, you would have thought that the President of the United States was there! I felt bad for the neighbors.

My parents were no longer living in the farmhouse I grew up in. They had sold it a few years ago and were now in a quiet community of connected townhouses. This was definitely the most action the semi-retirement community had seen in quite a while. With everyone loaded into their vehicles, the police-escorted procession began to make its way to the cathedral. While my dad seemed like a regular guy to me, he was not seen as such by everyone else.

Upon arriving at the church, it was evident that he was anything but typical. Hundreds of people were lined up by the crowd barriers; in fact, there were people *everywhere*! Large speakers had been erected outside so the audio portion of the service could be played over the speakers for those who were not able to get into the church. (A few days prior, my mom and I had decided to not allow people to take videos inside the church.)

Upon exiting the limos, all eight children and my mom gathered by the hearse that carried my dad's coffin. The six sons served as pallbearers behind bagpipe players as we entered the cathedral, awaited by more than two thousand people, with standing room only.

One thing that really struck me was how quiet all those people were. I wasn't expecting the roar of fans like at Memorial Stadium in the 1950s and '60s, but the silence was truly deafening. The coffin we carried down the long aisle to the front of the altar was blanketed with white lilies and roses.

Prior to the funeral mass we had a memorial service. Earlier that week my mom had called former Baltimore Colts wide receiver Raymond Berry and asked him to speak at my dad's funeral on behalf of the team. He graciously delivered this eulogy to the crowd, which included NFL Commissioner Paul Tagliabue, Baltimore Ravens coaches Ted Marchibroda and Brian Billick, and players Ray Lewis, Peter Boulware, and Michael McCrary:

Figure 4.3   Dad sharing a laugh with Raymond Berry in the 1990s.

For all of us who were fortunate to be a part of the Baltimore Colts—whether as team members or fans—by now we all realize it was a once-in-a-lifetime experience. And all of us know that the main reason was John Unitas, a once-in-a-lifetime quarterback. I think I can safely speak for all of us in saying, Thank you, John. You elevated us to unreachable levels—both on the field and in the stands. You made the impossible possible. You filled our memory bank full. Those images of your performances are still there and will never fade.

But you did more than perform on the field. Individual achievements and glory didn't have a place on your priority list. All of us knew you were focused on moving the ball into the end zone and winning the game. You didn't care who did what. Just do our jobs when called on, and we all win together. The Colts were a team, and your example and leadership set the tone.

Football is a physical game. Even in that respect, you set a tone and were a leader and an example. Personally, I think toughness was your number one asset. Not just physical—the hits you took—but mental toughness. You just kept on coming at 'em. In a different body, you would have been an ideal middle linebacker. All of us are glad God gave you the body to be a quarterback.

I guess it is appropriate at this time to thank the Lord, not only for your talent, but for sending you to Baltimore to bless all of us. You were more than a teammate to me. You were a special friend. And I came to love you like a brother. Because of your lifelong faith in Christ, you now have experienced the truth of the scripture—to be absent with the body is to be present with the Lord.

So, as we come here today to thank God for what you mean to each of us, and to celebrate your life, we don't question his timing. But we are going to miss you, Johnny U.

Janice, Paige, and I also eulogized our father. Speaking to thousands of people about my dad was one of the most difficult things I have ever done. I remember looking to my right from the pulpit and seeing my dad's Colts teammates. They were seated in a special section, on the side of the altar. It was hard to see them crying, these men who were like uncles to my siblings and me, and heroes to so many in attendance. This is the eulogy I gave that day:

In life we cross paths with many different people. Some we meet in passing, some through business, and others through friends and family. While all of these people are important, I have been taught and believe that the most important is family. Family, for me, extends beyond parents, brothers, sisters, and relatives. It extends to those other people who I love and whose opinions and thoughts I hold close to my heart. It includes those people who have been there from the beginning, until now. When times are tough and there is no sun in sight, there is always a select group of people who I can look to for love and support. All of these people are family to me.

Over the years, my father has been called a lot of things: Johnny U, The Golden Arm, Number 19, the GOAT. There are probably some other names he was called by my mom, but they should not be said here in church. During my lifetime my mom, brothers, sisters, relatives, and the rest of the family, who I alluded to a moment ago, have known him by only two names: Dad or John. I am here today to honor the life of my father.

In the 1999 HBO documentary UNITAS, my father said he did not get emotional over football games. The things that made him emotional were family, children, and animals. With that statement the viewers were given an inside look at who my dad really was and what he was all about. If you will permit me, I would like to share a few stories about my father and who he was.

It has been said by a lot of people that my father was a good motivator of men and that he could get them to do things with just a few words or sometimes even with one look. I have also heard that one possible reason for this was their fear of letting him down. A few years ago, the chimney of our old house was struck by lightning and exploded, leaving pieces of red brick and cement strewn across the roof of the house and lawn below.

One day my dad was ready to clean the roof off and he asked our good friend and neighbor, Ray Koontz, to help him remove all the rubble. Without hesitation Mr. Ray agreed to help. I am not sure how long it took them to clean the roof off, but I am sure to Mr. Ray it seemed like forever. You see, Mr. Ray is afraid of heights, so walking around on a roof was probably the last thing he wanted to do. When they finished, someone mentioned to Dad that Mr. Ray is afraid of heights. When Dad asked him why he didn't say something, Mr. Ray replied, "I didn't want you to have to do it alone."

Dr. Sam Havrilak, who is here today, along with his wife Terry and son Michael, was a wide receiver and teammate of my dad's from 1969 to 1972. After retiring, my dad and Dr. Havrilak remained friends. The Unitas and Havrilak families are very close friends. My brother Chad and Michael are the same age. When they were elementary school–aged, they spent many summers playing golf and tennis at Hillendale Country Club, where they were also on the swim team together.

I remember hearing a story about Chad, who was probably nine or ten at the time, so, late 1980s, spending the night at the Havrilaks' home. They lived approximately twenty minutes from us. In the very early morning hours of two or three a.m., Chad went into Dr. and Mrs. Havrilak's room and told Dr. Havrilak that he was not feeling good and wanted to go home. Sam called and woke my dad and told him that Chad wanted to go home. Dad's response was "Not a problem—you can bring him home."

After hanging up the phone, Sam began to get dressed. Mrs. Havrilak was awake at this point and asked her husband what he was doing. "I'm taking Chad home. He doesn't feel well." Mrs. Havrilak, a bit puzzled, asked, "Why are you taking him home?" to which Dr. Havrilak responded, "Because John said to."

The Grimm family—John and Claudia, along with their children Amy, Russell, and Molly—have been friends of ours dating back to when I was in elementary school. My mom and Mrs. Grimm met years ago at Hillendale Country Club while watching my brother Chad and Mrs. Grimm's son Russell play in the baby pool together. Their friendship evolved to the point where the

Grimms asked my parents to be godparents for their third child, Molly.

A few months after Molly was born my mom offered to watch her for the day so Mrs. Grimm could have some time to herself. Mrs. Grimm accepted and left Molly with my mom. When Mrs. Grimm returned home, she was shocked to find my mom had left and in her place was my dad. He was on the couch gently holding Molly in his big hands. My dad explained that my mom had left a couple hours ago. He had fed and changed Molly and was enjoying looking after her. He loved you, Molly, and other children so much that he would jump at the opportunity to be around them or help them.

I wanted to write something about my father because he was always, along with you, Mom, a big fan of anything that I wrote. One liberty I have granted myself as the writer and speaker is that I get to tell two personal stories about my dad.

The first deals with the support that he has always shown me with anything and everything I have ever done. As some of you know, I moved to Los Angeles a few years ago to pursue a career in acting. This decision came on the heels of five years in college and tens of thousands of dollars spent on my education. For those years of college, I have a bachelor's degree in sports administration to show for my efforts. Before I moved to California, I spent one year working for Tony Agnone at Eastern Athletic Services, a football agency here in town. I was actually using my degree!

During the spring of that year my father and I went to Dallas and worked on a movie called Any Given

Sunday. *Despite being in other movies, television shows, and countless commercials, Dad found the work extremely boring and of zero interest to him. The only reason he did it was because he knew that I was interested in movies, and if he did it, I could have a part alongside him in the film. When our time on the movie was over, we came back to Baltimore, and I began to think about moving to California. After about two weeks, I decided to take my five years of education and sports administration degree to Hollywood to become an actor.*

Most fathers would tell their son to forget it, and then ask for a refund on that college education, because they obviously didn't learn anything. My dad had a different response. He told me, "If that is what you want to do, then do it. Follow your heart and work hard. If you do, you can accomplish anything you want. Just remember that your mother and I will always be here to help and support you." The love and support that he showed that day, and continued to show each and every day until his passing, is a gift that could never be measured.

The second story I want to tell you just happened on Wednesday, the day he passed away. My dad had a reputation for being very straightforward. With him, things were always black or white, right or wrong. Mr. Bill Curry, a Colts teammate and center, remembers him for his pre-game speech that was always the same: "Talk is cheap—let's go play."

One month ago, my fiancée Dianna, her five-year-old son Clark, and I were here at the farmhouse for our wedding shower. The last day we were here I gave my mom a copy of a short film script I had written. I wanted her and

Dad to read it and let me know their thoughts. As I mentioned earlier, Dad was always a big fan of things I wrote and looked forward to reading anything I came up with.

As Mom and I were talking about Dad, I brought up the script. I never got a chance to ask him if he liked it, so I asked her what he said. She told me he said it was crap, and he didn't like it. He wanted me to write something better, because he knew I could.

Dad, I want you to know that this is the latest thing I have written. While you will never be able to read it, I know you're here listening to me read it. I hope you like this better. I love you and will miss you forever. Thank you.

When I'd finished my eulogy, I received an unexpected round of applause. Since this was a full mass, hymns, prayers, and communion followed.

As the ceremony ended, we all filed out of the cathedral. Just as we got to the steps, a plane flew over, as if choreographed for that precise moment, trailing a banner that read *Unitas We Stand*. This was the same plane that had flown the same banner when my dad threw his final touchdown in Memorial Stadium. That, too, could not have been planned to the exact minute, as the pilot had no idea what would be happening at the time of his flight over the stadium. It was meant to be.

Following the funeral service there was a private reception for family, friends, and teammates. One person I was surprised to see was former Miami Dolphins quarterback Dan Marino. Dan is from Pittsburgh, just like

Dad, and he got to know him very well over the years through many events and the work they did together. It meant a lot to me and my family that he traveled from his home in Florida to attend the funeral and pay his respects.

Looking back twenty-plus years later, it's hard to believe all that went into coordinating the funeral service. I met a lot of the leaders of Baltimore city and county government, members of the Baltimore city and county police departments, and people from the Baltimore Archdiocese. It was a huge team effort, one that Dad would have been proud of.

One of the most important lessons I had learned throughout my life, ingrained in me by my dad, was *Be a leader, not a follower.* It was clear at his funeral that my father had passed this valuable lesson on to countless others, as well.

* * *

It will forever amaze me, the respect and love this country has for my dad. Former players like Joe Montana of the San Francisco 49ers: "I played golf with John at the Crosby when it was in North Carolina. Our paths had crossed many times in the past, but this was the first time I actually spent an entire day with him. Prior to teeing off on the first tee, I told him that I had purchased a Unitas jersey, something I don't normally do. When I told John, he said, 'Why didn't you just call me—I would have given you one.' For me, personally, it was a great day!"

Joe was asked if he thought he (Joe) could play in the era of the 1950s and if John could play in the era of the 1990s. His response: "Sure! I think I could have played in his time and John in mine. Of course, the game has changed some, but all in all, it's still football. Neither one of us would struggle with it."

Former Baltimore receiver Jimmy Orr once said, "I played two years in the 1950s. I believe pro football was the toughest it ever was [then]. They didn't have any rules. I once saw a defensive guy kick a tight end in the face. No flag. They could bury your ass and not call it a penalty. Roughing the quarterback? Forget it!"

Jim Brown once said of my dad, "John could play anytime [any era]."

Peyton Manning said, "I wore black high-tops at Tennessee because of him. When I met John, I gave him a pair. My father's [Archie Manning] sports heroes were Mickey Mantle and Johnny U. At home I have a wall of photos, me posing with quarterbacks: Starr, Staubach, younger guys, too—Marino, Aikman, Favre. But the one of Unitas holding up the black high-tops is my favorite."

Similar to my dad, Peyton is adamant about completing his fake after the ball is gone. "Looking at highlight films I could see what a technician Unitas was. He cared about the smallest details. So do I. It's the little things that make the big difference. Timing is one of the most important parts of the game, and John was the best at it.

How does Peyton compare himself to my dad? "I make no comparison with myself to him. I hold John in such high regard that it is an honor just to wear the same uniform as him. The fact that my number is one below his and the fact that I wear the same horseshoe helmet, inspired me. He was the ultimate field general. He called his own plays and was in complete control out there. Aggressive. Fearless. Utterly fearless. He was convinced that if you did things right and had worked on them, it didn't matter what the situation was. He could make the play work."

OUR WEDDING DAY

One of the first things Mom told me when Dianna and I arrived in Baltimore for the funeral was that dad's passing was no reason to cancel or postpone our wedding. It was scheduled for September 28, 2002, just eleven days after the funeral. "Dad was looking forward to the wedding," Mom said, "and after this week, the family will need something to celebrate."

Fortunately, all the plans for the wedding had been made far in advance—the wedding venue, guest list, food, and reception—which made the next week and a half relatively stress-free. All we needed to do was pick up various items—tables, chairs, beverages, food—for the wedding and decorate the reception venue.

Following our engagement, Dianna and I had discussed the size of the wedding. Since her first wedding was large—and I wasn't particularly fond of big get-togethers, unless it's a Ravens game—we quickly agreed on an intimate ceremony in California with immediate family and close friends.

My mom, grandmother (Granny), Chad, Paige, and Georgia, our housekeeper (and "second momma") arrived in Long Beach on Thursday, September 26. The following day we had a brief wedding rehearsal at the Earl Burns Miller Japanese Garden on the campus of Long Beach State University. We chose the location for its beautiful setting, and because it was very close to the home Dianna and I were sharing. Located on the northwest corner of the campus, the garden is a hidden gem that features a large koi pond with a wooden bridge, winding pathways, a teahouse, and a Zen garden. Dianna and I both love its serenity and beauty.

Following the rehearsal, we moved on to Shoreline Village for the rehearsal dinner at Parkers' Lighthouse, which sits on the water's edge of Queensway Bay in downtown Long Beach. After dinner Dianna and I parted ways for the night. She went back to the house, and I went to stay at a hotel with my family.

The following morning was very relaxing. Mom, Paige, and Georgia went to Dianna's house, where all the women were getting dressed and having their hair and makeup done. That left Chad and I together to chill and watch college football before heading over to the garden.

The guest list was small, probably fifty people. This included immediate family: Dianna's mom and dad, three of her older siblings, cousins, and sisters-in-law; close friends from Dianna's work; my Baltimore lacrosse buddies; Melanie, my first roommate in LA, and her husband, Evan; Mr. and Mrs. Carnegie. And the one who had gotten my journey to California started, Maryellen, and her husband, Tommy.

Prior to the ceremony, Dianna and I presented a single rose to my mom, which she placed on the empty seat next to her in honor of my dad. Dianna's friend Irma served as her maid of honor, and her three nieces were flower girls. Chad was my best man, and Dianna's son Clark was the ring bearer. He also escorted Dianna down the path to the bridge where we stood for the ceremony. Short and sweet, it lasted maybe thirty minutes, and included Paige

Figure 4.4   With family on our wedding day. Left to right: Granny, Chad, Paige, Dianna, Clark, Joe, Mom, Georgia.

Figure 4.5   Our wedding ceremony on September 28, 2002.

reading a letter I had written to Dianna—a wedding-day surprise for her.

After the ceremony, we knocked out some family photos and then moved on to Dianna's brother's home for the reception, located only five houses down the street from ours. The neighborhood we all lived in was across the street from the Long Beach State University campus. We chose her brother's home because of the beautiful backyard that features a lattice-covered redbrick patio, trees, flowers, and two koi ponds. It was a perfect transition from the Japanese garden to his home.

The reception was extremely relaxed, with everyone being able to talk and socialize. Dianna and I really enjoyed the day, getting to spend quality time with all the guests and family. Dad was deeply missed, but definitely not forgotten. We felt his presence in the words of family and friends and stories shared. I know he would have enjoyed the day, because nothing was more important to him than his family and close friends. Lesson learned and executed on our wedding day, September 28, 2002.

BECOMING A DAD

Over the course of the next two years, I continued to pursue an acting career—auditioning, performing in plays, and studying at Playhouse West. To help support Dianna and Clark, I worked two part-time jobs: I was a substitute teacher for the Long Beach School District and a college recruitment advisor with College Bound Student Athletes.

Then, in late summer of 2004, Dianna and I learned that we were about to become parents. The baby was due in April 2005. I realized that I had come to a cross-roads in my life and a decision had to be made. I could no longer be selfish and think solely about *my* dream of being an actor. The part-time jobs were not going to give us the financial stability I wanted to provide for our growing family. Dianna and I shared the goal of owning our own home and having more children. While Dad's words—*Don't quit*—were echoing in my head, so were the words *Family first*. Over the next few months, I tried to find full-time employment, but, with a limited network, it proved difficult. At the same time Dianna and I began discussing the possibility of moving back east to

Baltimore, where finding full-time employment would be much easier.

This was a difficult decision to make. Dianna would be leaving her home and all of her family. We would also be taking Clark away from his father. This hurt the most, and I felt horrible doing it, but I knew in the long run that it would be the best decision for our family.

At the start of 2005, I flew back to Baltimore to begin searching for a job. I reached out to Steve Bisciotti, our family friend and owner of the Baltimore Ravens, to see if there were any potential opportunities with the team. It would be nice to actually use my college degree! He, in turn, hooked me up with the chief sales officer. It turned out that there were not any openings in the Ravens' sales department. However, I was informed that the Ravens were in the market for a new radio broadcast partner, and it was looking like WBAL-AM (a news radio station) and WIYY-FM (a rock radio station) would be that partner.

I was advised to look into possible employment in the radio sales departments where I would have the opportunity to cross-sell Ravens advertising packages with their account executives. It's not *what* you know, it's *who* you know. This proved to be spot on with the radio station.

Our neighbors when we lived on the farm were Ray and Nora Koontz (Mr. Ray from the roof story). "Miss Nora" worked for WBAL-AM for over twenty years and was the top sales executive year in and year out. Remember Molly Grimm, my parents' goddaughter? Her mom,

Claudia, was a high-performing sales executive with WBAL as well. WIYY-FM (98 Rock), the sister station to WBAL, had an opening for an account executive.

I submitted my résumé, and after what I'm sure were some positive words from Miss Nora and Mrs. Grimm, I was able to get an initial phone interview with the 98 Rock sales manager Hughes Jean in March 2005. Shortly after that, I flew back to Maryland where I interviewed with Hughes, WBAL sales manager Arthur Hawkins, and Bob Cecil, sales director for both stations.

My sales experience was limited to a summer job in college and part-time with College Bound Student Athletes. I didn't have any experience in media marketing/advertising. I don't typically get nervous in pressure situations, a Unitas trait, but I was extremely nervous on the day of the interviews. This was going to be a major life change for Dianna, Clark, and me if the interviews went well and led to an employment offer.

I left the interviews feeling good. The conversations went well, and I was told by Hughes that he would let me know in the next few days. I left the offices and went to the airport to fly back to California. Little did I know that this would become my routine for the summer of 2005.

A few days after returning to California I received a call from Hughes offering me the job. Since Dianna was due in mid- to late April, a projected start date was set for early May.

Dianna had routine checkups throughout the pregnancy, and everything was going smoothly. She and the baby were both healthy. It was on her last checkup that the sonographer informed us the baby was in breech position. Because it was so late in the pregnancy, the delivery would have to be induced. It was scheduled for April 22.

The obstetrician told us that a procedure called external cephalic version (ECV) could be attempted, in an effort to turn the baby into a head-down position so a normal vaginal birth could occur. The doctor would gently push on the abdomen to get the baby to move. We were informed that most of the time this is successful, but if not, a C-section would be required.

The way the doctor made this sound and the reality of the procedure are polar opposites! First of all, the doctor who came into the room looked like he had just come from Muscle Beach in Venice, California. He was tan, his hair was perfect, and he had arms like the Ultimate Warrior. He explained to us that he was going to take Dianna's belly in his hands and try to turn the baby. He told me to hold Dianna's hand, because it wasn't going to be comfortable—definitely an understatement. This was the day I learned Dianna is way tougher than I'll ever be.

It was super painful for her. So much so that she seemed to be crying and laughing at the same time. I'm not sure if "You motherf*****" was directed at me or the doctor, but it was definitely said. The doctor was able to move the baby 45 degrees, but after the doctor let go, the baby returned to the breech position. One more unsuccessful attempt was made. At this point the baby's heart rate started to escalate, so the physicians decided it was time to proceed with the C-section.

Not long after all this craziness, we welcomed Colten John Unitas to the world. I was able to spend the next week with Dianna and our baby boy before traveling back to Baltimore to begin working at 98 Rock, on May 1. This was definitely the most conflicted time in my life. I was leaving my wife with our newborn son to start a new chapter in our life, without my family with me.

My mom stayed with Dianna for a couple of weeks, and Dianna's mother was also close by to help, but I still felt like I was making a huge mistake. I had to trust in what Dad had taught me about putting family first. From May until early August, I worked in Baltimore, Monday through Friday, flying back to California on Friday evening and taking the red-eye back to Baltimore on Sunday night.

THE MOVE TO BALTIMORE—MEMORIES, DISAPPOINTMENTS, AND DECISIONS
In early August 2005, we packed everything up into two U-Hauls and moved to Maryland. Technically, it wasn't "we." I had to work, and since Colten was only a few months old, there was no way we were driving him cross-country.

Whenever I need help, I know I can rely on my family. I hired Chad and my mom to be the drivers. Chad was accompanied by Clyde, our English bulldog. At the time we had a Ford Expedition that was coming back to

Maryland with us. We had to rent a trailer to carry the Expedition. Looking back on it, we probably should have put the SUV on a car hauler, but we didn't have a ton of extra money, so we did the best we could.

I've made the drive across the United States twice, east to west, and it's long! I would drive fourteen hours a day and make it in approximately three and a half days. Chad had never driven cross-country, and after doing so this time, I doubt he'll do it again.

In convincing him to take on the task, I told him it's an easy drive, basically all highways. Since it was summer, he wouldn't have to worry about the treacherous weather. I did omit the part about the trailer, however. Towing a trailer limits the speed at which one can drive. We paid him one thousand dollars—not nearly enough, but to a broke college kid, it was a lot. It would buy him a good amount of beer. (Big brothers are good at persuasion!)

Once mom and Chad began their cross-country trip, Dianna, Colten, and I headed to the airport for our flight to Baltimore. Clark stayed behind and spent his last few weeks of summer with his dad. We rented a townhome in Lutherville the first year. Oddly enough, it was only a five-minute walk from the original home I grew up in.

When I was a child, we lived at 311 West Timonium Road. Looking back at that property, I have so many fond memories. The house and property were awesome, approximately seven acres. The house was white with dark-blue shutters and sat at the top of a big hill, over-looking a neighborhood across the street. The driveway started at the bottom of the hill on Timonium Road and wound its way up the hill, almost a full S shape.

The property was surrounded by a large, wooded area on the sides, and rear. As kids we spent countless hours playing in the woods, riding our bikes, and walking the various paths with Mom and Dad. My mom loved gardening, tending to the numerous flower beds on the property. In the winter, when it snowed, lots of kids from the neighborhood across the street would come to our hill and go sledding.

Dad had a tractor with a plow (the one I ran over him with) to clear the driveway when it snowed. He would always leave a spot, roughly 10 yards wide, unplowed. This was the transition zone from the top of the hill to the bottom, probably around 120 yards, and you had to guide your sled or inner tube across this area.

Dad loved the property because of the quiet. He loved to ride the tractor and cut the grass, tending to the trees and the general upkeep of the property. He also enjoyed playing with Chad, Paige, and me. There was a side yard that served as the sports field, where we played football, soccer, lacrosse, and baseball. There were electric lines that crossed one end of the yard, and they served as the home-run wall or field goal, depending on the sport being played. Hit the ball over the wires, home run! Kick the ball over the wires, field goal is good!

The other end of the yard had a large, chain-link-fenced kennel area for the dogs. There was a massive doghouse, originally for Pro, the Saint Bernard my parents had when

I was born. Pro was massive. I could sit on his back and hold on to his collar and ride him like a horse when I was very young.

Over the years this fenced-in area would also be home to multiple rabbits, chickens, and Rugby, our lamb. Rugby was a surprise birthday gift my mom got from Dad's Colts teammate, Fred Miller.

We used to position our lacrosse goal a few yards in front of the fence because it made a great backstop for missed shots. Some of my favorite memories of that side yard are the one-on-one football games Chad and I played with Dad as the all-time quarterback. As kids we never looked at him as "Johnny U"; he was just Dad, playing with his sons. But there was one thing that made him different from other dads: His passes were perfect spirals, and always on target. Whenever Chad or I would drop a pass, we would hear, "What did you drop it for? I hit you right in the hands!"

The driveway was huge at the top of the hill, by the house. We had an in-ground basketball hoop where many games of H-O-R-S-E and one-on-one were played. At the far end of the driveway there was a freestanding garage where the tractor, push mowers, various yard tools, kids' bikes, outdoor toys, and countless balls were stored.

In the mid-1980s the wooded area behind the house was sold and developed for future townhomes—one of which Dianna and I would move into decades later. During the first eleven years we lived in our house, there were never any crime issues, but after the development started, there were a couple of attempted break-ins. That's why my family moved to the farm in 1987.

It was surreal to be back in Lutherville, married, with two children, and living just minutes from the original house I grew up in. The newness was exciting, but I was nervous about how Dianna would adapt to the East Coast, and how well Clark would make the transition once he arrived and started attending a new school where he would not know anyone.

One nice thing about being back in Maryland was the network of people we were immediately surrounded with. I was already working, but Dianna needed to find work as well. With the help of a few close family friends, Dianna was introduced to a woman named Heidi who was opening up a brand-new boutique called Fresh, just a few miles from where we lived. At the time, Dianna had close to twenty years' experience in women's fashion, in both sales and management. She was the perfect fit for Fresh.

After the building was completed on the store, Dianna went to work. She helped with everything— managing, purchasing, sales, and more. Heidi knew tons of people, a true social butterfly. She would get the customers to the store and Dianna would close the sale.

My mom lived just a couple miles from our home, so she and Georgia were a huge help watching Colten a few days a week for us. We also hired Molly Grimm (my parents' goddaughter) to help babysit Colten and Clark on days that Mom and Georgia were not able to help.

Work went well for both of us, and after our first year living in Maryland, we were able to purchase our first home together. The following year we welcomed another son, Casey, to the family.

While things were going well for our family—kids were healthy, Clark was doing well at school, making friends, and playing multiple sports—the opportunity to move from 98 Rock to the Baltimore Ravens never materialized. It was a lot to ask of Dianna to move all the way across the country and leave her entire family behind. Although she never came right out and said it, I knew it was hard for her to be away from her mom, as they shared a very close relationship. The mother–daughter bond between the two of them was strong, and she missed Jen tremendously.

By late 2007, I had left 98 Rock for a new job based on promises of higher pay and fast advancement opportunities that did not happen. With Dianna not being totally happy, and Clark almost 3,000 miles from his father, we decided it was time to move back out west.

Dianna and I wanted to be able to purchase a home right away, but we could not afford the Southern California real estate market. We also wanted to be close enough to her mom and Clark's dad so everyone could be together more often. The weather was also important. Baltimore winters are cold, gray, wet, icy, and depressing. Dianna and I both agreed that we didn't want anywhere cold. We decided that Las Vegas, Nevada, was the best place to accommodate all of our goals for raising the boys—closer

Figure 4.6   With Clark (far left), Colten, and Casey in Hollywood, 2022.

to family (only a four-hour drive or forty-five-minute flight to Long Beach), and great weather.

In June 2008 we sold our home and moved to Las Vegas. Clark and I took three days to drive cross-country with Clyde, and Dianna, Colten, and Casey flew out the day after we arrived in Las Vegas.

Overtime
A Tribute to Dad

THE SEED IS PLANTED

In the spring of 2003, a man reached out to my mom regarding making a movie about my dad's life. A couple of documentaries had been made in the past by HBO and ESPN, but never a feature film. When my dad was alive, he had been approached multiple times about making a movie, and his response was always the same: "Who in the hell would want to see that?" Another of his life's lessons—Stay humble!

This man, whose name I don't remember (he claimed to have been one of the writers on the film *61**, the story about Roger Maris's chase of Babe Ruth's home-run record), offered to travel from New York to meet with my mom and me. The only thing I remember about the meeting was the guy wanted $250,000 to write the screenplay. If my dad had been alive, he likely would have told the guy to shovel shit somewhere else.

After the man left, I told my mom, "Screw that guy! If we decide to make a movie, I'll write the screenplay myself." I headed back to Los Angeles, and we didn't discuss a movie about Dad again—until 2006.

JOHNNY U: THE LIFE AND TIMES OF JOHN UNITAS— THE BOOK

In 2006, the book *Johnny U: The Life and Times of John Unitas* was penned by author Tom Callahan. The book jacket introduces Tom as follows: "Tom Callahan, a former senior writer at *Time* magazine and sports columnist at the *Washington Post*, is a recipient of the National Headliner Award. He has covered three decades of everything in major league sports, from Sarajevo to Zaire, including hundreds of pro football games and numerous Super Bowls. Among his many *Time* cover subjects are San Francisco quarterback Joe Montana and Chicago running back Walter Payton. Callahan is the author of three other books, the most recent being *The Bases Were Loaded (and So Was I)*."

I would like to introduce Tom as a good, loyal friend of the Unitas family. In 1967, Tom was fresh out of college, working as the high school sports reporter for the *Evening Sun*. Back then, the *Baltimore Sun* printed two newspapers per day. The *Sun* was the morning edition, and the *Evening Sun* was, of course, the evening edition.

In the fall of 1967 Tom was assigned to do a sidebar story on the Colts. After a home game against the Chicago Bears, Tom was in the locker room where he was noticed by Raymond Berry. Tom explained to me, "Raymond came up to me and said, 'You're the *lostest*-looking guy in the room. What are you doing in here?'" Tom explained that he was assigned to do a sidebar story for the paper. "Who do you want to talk to?" said Berry. "John Unitas," Tom replied. Without hesitation, Raymond took Tom to my dad's locker, where he was surrounded by the beat reporters—*the real reporters*, as Tom described them to me.

Raymond reached over and grabbed my dad's arm and said, "John, I want you to meet my good friend Tom Callahan from the *Evening Sun*. He'd like to speak with you." Tom was laughing as he told me the story. " 'My good friend!' I had just met Raymond two minutes ago. Raymond slid a small stool over my way—the type of stool you would use to milk a cow—and John grabbed his stool. He sat with me and talked way longer than he should have. I was a nobody."

Dad was typically very guarded and not very trusting of the columnists who he felt were more about making themselves look good. He preferred the beat guys, Cameron Snyder and Larry Harris, who were there day in and day out. But if you were introduced by Raymond Berry or another close friend, you had a shot at getting to know the real Dad.

Tom would go on to say, "He used to call me Tommy. The only other person who ever called me Tommy was my mom. John was very loyal. If I called and left him a message, he would always call back. 'You *bull crappers* in the media—how ya doin,' Tommy?' was how he started every call with me."

A couple of years after Dad passed away, my mom was introduced to Tom by Ernie Accorsi, then general manager of the New York Giants. Mr. Accorsi was a longtime close, personal friend of our family. He started his career in 1970 with the Baltimore Colts as the PR director. He worked his way up through the front-office ranks and served as general manager of the Colts, Cleveland Browns, and the aforementioned New York Giants before retiring as the most senior GM in the National Football League in 2006.

Ernie and Tom became good friends over the years. Tom wanted to write a book about Dad. When Dad was alive, he never authorized such a book to be written, and neither had Mom since he had passed away. After learning about Tom's history with Dad, coupled with Ernie's recommendation, Tom was given the okay by Mom.

Johnny U: The Life and Times of John Unitas is the only family-approved biography of Dad. We all love the book. Tom went to great lengths to do his homework, speaking with family members, teammates, and close friends. He probably even talked to valets, waiters, and chefs about Dad, based on details in the book. What Tom produced is hands down the best, and most accurate, book ever written about my dad. I learned things about my own family that I never knew. *Johnny U* was a *New York Times* bestseller, and Tom's most successful book of all time.

Mom, Chad, Paige, and I were given advance copies of the book before it was published. I laughed, cried, reminisced, and learned a lot. After reading it, I knew the Unitas movie was within its pages.

The first thing I did was contact Tom to see if he would be gracious enough to grant me the rights to his book. I'll never forget what he said: "It's not my book. It's your dad's, and your family's. I was just lucky enough to be the guy who got to write it."

With the rights to the book in hand, I now had to figure out how to convert a 286-page book about an entire lifetime into a two-hour screenplay!

WRITING THE SCREENPLAY

When thinking about the story I wanted to tell, I knew it couldn't be just about football. That's boring. Anyone can go to YouTube and watch game films and highlights or look up stats on Pro Football Reference.

One thing that has always interested me is the backstory of successful people. It's great that they achieve success in their particular field, but what led to that success? Who supported them? What obstacles did they face? What drove him or her to never quit? After thinking about it, I knew *UNITAS* would be Dad's backstory. The following is a synopsis:

John Unitas is considered the godfather of the modern-day quarterback. He exploded onto the national scene on December 28, 1958, when he helped lead the Baltimore Colts to their first NFL World Championship. On that day, the Colts defeated the New York Football Giants in what has become known as the "Greatest Game Ever Played." This game, the first-ever nationally televised

NFL Championship, was watched by an audience of more than 40,000,000. Prior to the 2017 Super Bowl, it was the only World Championship / Super Bowl to be decided in sudden-death overtime.

Even though Unitas solidified his legacy that day as one of the greatest athletes to ever play the game, his part Rocky, part Rudy journey to stardom, and eventually the Pro Football Hall of Fame, was not an easy one.

UNITAS *tells the story of John's early life, from the age of five to twenty-five, and the pursuit of his childhood dream to become a professional football player.*

John Unitas grew up sharing a very small house with his three siblings, mother, father, and extended family in a poor section of Pittsburgh. Young John's father, who became ill from years of working in the Pennsylvania coal industry, died right in front of John when he was only five years old. John's older brother, Leonard, who was eleven years old at the time, quickly became the male role model for John.

In addition to attending school, Leonard took on work responsibilities with the family coal delivery business, to help support the family. Helen, John's mother, took on three jobs to support and provide for her family. The example set by Leonard and Helen regarding commitment, work ethic, and toughness would prove invaluable to John in his future pursuit of professional football, but would also be detrimental to his marriage and family.

John faced recurring rejection, along with questions regarding his size and ability to play, throughout his football career. Starting in middle school, through high school, college, and even his early years as a professional, John would repeatedly prove that "looks don't count."

In 1956, John was given a tryout and earned a roster spot with the Baltimore Colts. Over the next couple of years, John struggled to balance his faith, family, and football responsibilities. As the Colts were positioning themselves for a run at the 1958 NFL Championship, the unrest between John and his wife, Dorothy, threatened their marriage and family. John had to decide what was more important—his family, or the opportunity to become a world champion.

In the fall of 2006, I started outlining the script on a legal pad, which I actually still have. I've kept all the notes from the development of the script, including interviews with Colts teammates, my aunt Shirley, and my uncle Leonard (Dad's younger sister and older brother, respectively).

One day I called Raymond Berry with a couple of questions about the 1958 Championship Game. We ended up on the phone for two hours. He talked through every play of the drive to tie—and then win—the game. He still remembered the play calls.

One thing I've noticed is that elite-level athletes have amazing memories and can recall the smallest details of what they did, even if it was decades ago. I can't tell you what I did last week!

NICK SLATKIN—ACTOR AND SCREENWRITER
I have a hard copy of Tom's book with highlighted sections and countless notes in the margins. After a few weeks of pulling everything together, I began writing the script.

I couldn't have been more than a couple weeks into the project when I got a call from Nick Slatkin. I didn't know Nick personally, but he told me that he and my brother Chad were elementary school classmates at St. Paul's. He was living in Los Angeles, working as an actor and studying screenwriting at UCLA. He went on to tell me he had just finished reading this incredible book, *Johnny U*, about my dad, and he thought it would make for a great movie.

I told him I agreed. "In fact, I've been developing the story and script for the past few weeks," I said, adding that he was welcome to help me write the screenplay. Happily, Nick was interested. I sent him my outline, and soon, we had divided up the sections and gotten to work.

Working full-time and having a baby at home, I wasn't able to write for hours on end, so the process was slow. Still, after a few months we had our first draft. I don't remember exactly how long it was, but it was definitely over two hundred pages.

Movie scripts are usually anywhere from 90 to 120 pages. Rule of thumb: One minute of screen time equals one page of a script. Nick and I had agreed to put anything and everything into the first draft, knowing we would be cutting much of it over time as we fleshed out the story.

By the spring of 2007, we had finished our first draft, cutting it down to around 160 pages. It was time to let an expert read it and get feedback on more cuts and better story development.

Barry Levinson's Critique

That expert was Barry Levinson, who won a Best Director Oscar for the film *Rain Man*. He was a three-time Academy Award nominee for his screenwriting for *And Justice for All*, *Diner*, and *Avalon*.

Barry grew up in Baltimore watching my dad and the Colts play. He spent many days on the Western Maryland College (now, McDaniel College) campus, watching the Colts go through their summer camp practices, and many Sunday afternoons in Memorial Stadium. With his knowledge of this memorable era in Baltimore, coupled with his expertise in screenwriting, I couldn't think of a more qualified person to help us with the script. We understood that Barry had no business helping novices like us; his time is far too valuable to be spent reading our script. Ultimately, I know he did it out of respect for my father.

Over the next year or so, Barry was gracious enough to read two or three drafts. I would send the script to him via e-mail and then we would discuss it over the phone. He never rewrote lines or came up with new scenes. His notes were more focused on the overall development of the story and making the characters more human, more real. "Cut out as much football as possible," Barry advised. "Only use football as a bridge to the next stage of the story, and *only* if needed. The viewer needs to connect with the characters—show real-life experiences that someone in the audience can relate to. Create emotions— laughter, sadness, rage, et cetera."

Nick and I could never repay Barry for the time he gave us and the wisdom and advice he shared. Hopefully he will enjoy the movie and be able to reminisce about his time as a young boy in Baltimore, watching his beloved Colts.

One thing I've learned about screenwriting is that it's never really finished. There are countless changes that can be made. Scenes can be rewritten; lines can be delivered by different characters; the setting for the scene can be changed to make it more dramatic. Even when the movie is in production, changes can still be made to the script.

Case in point: I was in two Garry Marshall movies, *The Princess Diaries* and *Raising Helen*. Every day of production, while Garry was directing, he had at least two writers sitting right behind him. The writers were constantly writing jokes or making changes to lines in the script. They would rip pieces of paper from their legal pads with the new joke or line and pass it to Garry. If Garry liked it, he would pass it on to the actor to use in the next take.

The computer I used when I began writing *UNITAS* is long gone, so I don't have every draft of the script. My records date back to 2012, and the current count is fifty-eight drafts. Some of the rewrites are as small as a scene or two, while others are complete blow-ups and start-overs.

The one thing that has never changed is that we are telling Dad's backstory, and the movie ends at the 1958 Colts vs. Giants NFL Championship . . . unless we decide to do a rewrite. Hey, as Dad always said, "Don't quit!"

THE NIGHTMARE OF PRODUCING AND FINANCING

I have never attempted to raise a significant amount of money in my professional life. I'd never written a screenplay before, either. So why not tackle two things I have zero experience with, back to back? Sounds like fun. Actually, the screenwriting is fun; raising investment capital, not so much.

According to Americanfilmmakers.com, "Of the 3,715 feature films released between 2000–2025, 41 percent made a profit while 59 percent did not. The genres most likely to turn a profit were animation, horror, and adventure, while crime, drama, and biographies fared the worst."

So, here I am, a first-time screenwriter and producer, trying to raise tens of millions in investment capital for a dramatic sports biopic film that, historically, has a nearly 60 percent failure rate. I knew that financing a movie was difficult, but I didn't know the statistical reality.

By 2012, when I started working on film financing, I was already six years in, so my mind was already made up. As Dad always said, "Once I make my mind up, you might as well get out of my way!"

Over the past twelve years, I've met and spoken with more bullshitters than I can count. I have a five-page, single-spaced document with names of producers, investors, angel investors, fund managers, family office managers, investment bankers, and some randoms, who all at one point said they could put the money together to finance the film. Each group's level of interest lasted from a couple of weeks to the longest, over six years.

I traveled to Palo Alto, California, for two days of meetings with an Asian investor who was showing real promise. That was until a few weeks later when he asked to meet again, but during this encounter, requested that I pay for hotel rooms and cars for his investment partners while they stayed in Los Angeles. Pound sand, pal!

There was another potential investor who said he could put together $10 million by selling off some land in the Amazon rainforest. I've had two separate instances— one with a Russian, and the other, a guy from New York—where multiple calls and meetings were exchanged and then all of a sudden, they vanished. The best part of this story is that each of those men reached out to me a couple of years later, both saying they had spent the past couple of years in prison. One did his time in Mexico, and the other in Russia. I wish I had known earlier; I would have connected the two of them so they could be pen pals!

One of my favorite (not really) investment scenarios is the 50/50 match. Basically, the investor says he or she will match 50 percent of the money invested, but they won't be the first to put money in. Thanks, but no thanks!

All of these individuals have one thing in common: They have produced zero money in the bank. Dealing with these folks has been draining and discouraging.

I know; it's more than likely these people were all full of shit, but I had to take each one seriously, at least at the beginning, because one of them might have actually turned out to be real.

Over the years I've gotten much better at sniffing out the true bullshitters. The one thing they all have in common is that they talk more about themselves than anything else, at the rate of a mile a minute, typically saying nothing beneficial to the conversation. I keep telling myself that it took my dad close to fifteen years to realize his dream of becoming a professional football player, so I guess I still have a few years to go before I match him.

BREAKING DAD'S RECORD

With innumerable passing records and numerous championships, my dad became the model for the modern-day quarterback, as well as a model for consistency. I guess you could say that he was the National Football League's version of Major League Baseball's Joe DiMaggio. My dad always said that whenever he was playing, he was consistent, and the team always got 1,000 percent out of him.

On December 4, 1960, my dad threw a touchdown pass in his forty-seventh consecutive game—a record that stood for over fifty years. Before that, Cecil Isbell had held the record with a streak of twenty-three games, which was established in 1942.

Many great quarterbacks have passed through the league, but none came within even ten games of my dad's streak. Then, from 2009 to 2012, Drew Brees did what many thought was impossible. On September 30, 2012, Drew threw a touchdown pass against the Green Bay Packers which tied the record.

I sent Drew an e-mail that night, wishing him well in breaking my dad's record:

Drew,

I wanted to take a minute to congratulate you on tying my father's record of most consecutive games with a touchdown pass. My father always said that records were meant to be broken. The things that he would appreciate most about you have nothing to do with football. It's about who you are as a person. You're a role model for today's youth, a family man, and a humanitarian who cares for his community.

My father would tell you that these are the most important things in life, not some record in a book. My family and I will be watching Sunday night, cheering for you. Best of luck.

Sincerely,
Joe Unitas

I wrote the e-mail because I wanted him to know my family and I were proud of him, and we supported his breaking the record. While I'd never intended for it to become public, that's exactly what happened.

My phone started buzzing with texts and calls the next morning, starting around 7:00 a.m. Pacific time. I ignored the first few calls because I didn't recognize the numbers. One of the texts said, "Nice letter." I wasn't sure what that meant because I had no idea my e-mail had become public. I hadn't even told anyone about it.

Most of that morning was spent fielding calls and texts from the media across the country. On Wednesday of that week, I was contacted by a producer from NBC's *Football Night in America*. I was asked if I would be willing to attend the Sunday-night game in New Orleans. I was honored to be asked to represent my family at the game, and flew to New Orleans on Friday.

It was surprising to know just how much Drew and my dad had in common. Neither one was a top draft pick or came to camp with high expectations. My dad was cut by the Steelers, and Drew was let go by the Chargers after five seasons. Ironically, Drew was set to play San Diego that Sunday night. Both men have stories that are worthy of a Hollywood film.

On Saturday afternoon I was taken to the Saints' practice facility where I had the opportunity to meet Drew and spend a few minutes with him. I told him about the screenplay and that I had to change the ending. It originally stated that most of Dad's records had been broken, except for one, the forty-seven games with a TD pass. I changed the ending, prior to the game, to say it took over fifty years for the record to be broken. I told Drew, "Don't make me change it back."

During my dad's Hall of Fame speech, he said, "A man never gets to this station in life without being helped, aided, shoved, and pushed in doing something the proper way." With three minutes to go in the first quarter, Drew stepped back and threw the record-breaking touchdown.

On the night that my dad's record was broken, number 19 seemed to be everywhere in the stadium. The record-breaking touchdown went to number 19, Devery Henderson. Drew's second touchdown pass was for 19 yards. You can't make this stuff up! The spirit of my dad came through loud and clear that night. It showed in Drew's will to win.

My dad once said, "I never knew that I was throwing touchdown passes in every ball game and setting some kind of a record. I don't look at the record books. All I cared about was if we won!" Drew threw 4 touchdowns that night with a come-from-behind win in the second half after rallying his team from a 10-point deficit. I couldn't have written it better myself.

GARY HUDSON AND TIM MOORE

Throughout my years of writing and fund-raising, I always kept in touch with my close friend Gary Hudson. Somewhere between 2015 and 2016 Gary told me he was friends with a gentleman by the name of Tim Moore. They had gotten to know each other on the set of the movie *Road House* (1989). Tim was the executive producer, while Gary played one of the bouncers in the film.

Tim is a well-respected producer who has worked side by side with Clint Eastwood at his production company, Malpaso Productions, since 2002. During this time, he has been credited as line producer, coproducer, producer, and executive producer. Gary reached out to Tim and told him about me and the *UNITAS* script. After reading it, Tim was interested and agreed to a meeting.

We met at the Malpaso Productions office on the Warner Bros. studio lot. Tim, being a huge football fan (49ers) and a fan of my dad, believed in my story and agreed to help produce the film. At this time, Mr. Eastwood was still directing roughly one film per year; therefore, the amount of time Tim could give to *UNITAS* depended on which stage of production he was at with his current Malpaso project.

I was humbled by the fact that Tim was willing to help. It was nice to finally have someone real, who knew the business side of Hollywood, to help steer the project forward. Trying to put together a movie is like trying to piece together a jigsaw puzzle. First of all, you need a great deal of money for financing. Next, you need a director. A top director can attract star lead actors, followed by supporting actors, day players (actors who work for a few days), and a massive crew to coordinate and execute the daily production of the film. Depending on the size of the film, it usually takes around one to one and a half years to make a film, beginning with preproduction to the actual release of the film.

The film's producer handles the film, from inception to completion. This includes coordinating the planning; hiring the cast, the director, and the editor; and overseeing the finances, marketing, and distribution. Basically, the producer manages the entire film production process. So far, I have found the most challenging part of producing to be securing the financing while also trying to attach a top director and star actor. This process is akin to the age-old question of what came first, the chicken or the egg?

DIRECTOR DAVID ANSPAUGH

Speaking of directors, back in 2006 there were two at the top of my list: Barry Levinson and David Anspaugh. David is responsible for two of the most beloved sports dramas in the history of cinema, *Hoosiers* (1986) and *Rudy* (1993).

Both men were long shots, and, of course, in high demand. Some may not realize it, but A-level actors' and directors' schedules are usually booked out with projects a couple of years in advance. Although he would have been great, Barry's schedule just wouldn't allow it. I don't remember how it happened, but I was able to track down David Anspaugh a couple of years after moving to Las Vegas, likely in 2010 or 2011. I left him a voicemail and he called me back.

David was born in 1946 in Decatur, Indiana, and was a big basketball fan. This was long before the Colts moved to Indiana, so, at the time, Indiana was 100 percent a basketball state. In 1958 David's father, Lawrence, took him to the Colts–Giants NFL Championship Game. "That's the day I fell in love with football," David told me, "and Johnny U became my sports hero." From that day on, whenever the Colts played a game within driving distance or by train within the state of Indiana, David and his dad would go to see them play.

Getting back to the phone call . . . At the time we spoke, David had stopped directing and was teaching film classes at Indiana University. Because of this, he wouldn't be in a position to direct *UNITAS*. However, he offered to read the script and even provided some notes and insight on what Nick and I could do to further improve the screenplay. I kept in touch with David over the years to see if his teaching status had changed, and if he might be willing to direct. He was gracious but always unable to accept the offer.

This all changed in the fall of 2022. Unbeknownst to me, David was no longer teaching at Indiana University when I called him that fall. We caught up, and I updated him on the trials of attaching a director for the project. Although he wasn't teaching, David wasn't sure if he was at a stage where he wanted to dedicate a year of his life to a film, so he passed on the offer. I told him I understood and would continue looking.

It wasn't more than a week later that David rang me back and asked if the offer to direct was still available. Of course it was! We talked further about the script; he had some ideas, and wanted to know if I was open to changes.

Being raised by one of the humblest men out there, and being the furthest thing from a professional writer, I have always been open to help in developing a better script.

David wanted to make some changes of his own, and also wanted to have a writer friend of his, "PC," whom he had worked with in the past, help with those changes. David still lived in Indiana but would be in Los Angeles for Thanksgiving. The following day, David, PC, Gary, Tim, and I got together.

It was nice to finally meet David in person after all the years of speaking on the phone. The meeting lasted a few hours. We discussed the script, shared stories, and had the opportunity to hear about how *Hoosiers* came together. While it was okay for changes to be made, we all agreed that Nick and I would have final script approval. We all left the meeting feeling good about where we were heading with the script, and I was personally very excited to have the man who directed two of the best sports dramas ever at the helm of *UNITAS*.

Over the course of the next few months, David and PC worked on the script, and by mid-March 2023, they were finished. After reading the script, Tim, Gary, Nick, and I gathered all of our notes together and then reconnected with PC. Further changes were made by PC and me, and by early April the script was finished.

The overall story didn't change much, although the sequencing of how the story is told did. I think the biggest change, for the better, came in the development of the characters and bringing more life to the era. One of the more recent compliments I've received on the script was, "It's like a Norman Rockwell painting came to life."

Finally, the project was starting to pick up steam. We had a script everyone felt great about. Our director was on board. The "package" was coming together, allowing us to make presentations to studios, streaming platforms, and independent financiers.

Then all at once, it came to an abrupt stop.

I received a call from David in the later part of April. He told me that for personal reasons, he wouldn't be able to direct the film. I could tell in his voice that he was heartbroken. He had been so excited about the script and was looking forward to directing the film. I, too, was heartbroken that we'd lost our director.

The great thing about life is you get to control your own destiny. In this particular situation, I could feel bad and be depressed that we lost David, or I could be happy that he and PC had done a great job and helped us develop an even better script. When I was young and my team lost a game, I would sometimes hang my head and sulk. Dad was usually there when I came off the field, and he would say "Pick your chin up." He wouldn't stand for self-pity. I was supposed to be proud of the effort put forth in competition, regardless of the outcome, and to display that in how I carried myself.

I felt bad for David, but not myself. Because of him, I had a better script. I was ready to keep trying.

It *Really* Doesn't Cost Anything to Be Nice

In the fall of 2023, I watched a show on Netflix called *King of Collectibles.* This show is about Ken Goldin, the owner of an auction house in New Jersey that specializes in the auctioning of sports memorabilia and pop culture items.

My dad never cared much about the trophies and awards he had accumulated over the years. Winning was always the most important thing, and as we know, he only got emotional about family and animals. In fact, to show just how little he thought of the trophies, my mom found them in boxes out by the side of the road for the trash man to pick up—twice! She, of course, grabbed the boxes and brought them back into the house.

After my parents downsized from the farmhouse to the townhouse, there wasn't room enough to display all his trophies. So, in March 2002, my parents decided to donate most of the memorabilia to the Sports Legends Museum in Baltimore. At the ceremony, Dad said, "I think this stuff should be here. This is where I played all these years. The people of Baltimore have always been very gracious to me." There were some more meaningful items, such as championship rings, high-tops, uniform pieces, and a few select trophies that my mom convinced my dad to hold on to. These items remained in storage containers for the next twenty-two years.

After watching the show, I contacted my mom and told her that we needed to do something with the pieces she still had. My siblings and I didn't want the memorabilia, and the pieces were gathering dust in storage. The four of us came to a mutual decision that it was time to sell the items and use the proceeds to help others via charitable contributions.

After consulting with individuals close to the family (former players who played with my dad) who have also auctioned off their personal memorabilia, we decided to entrust the items to Hunt Auctions. David Hunt and his team lived up to their reputation as being among the finest vintage sports memorabilia auctions in the country. Every year, in conjunction with the NFL, Hunt Auctions hosts a live event the day before the Super Bowl. A portion of the proceeds from the auction go to benefit many NFL charities. Fortunately, the 2024 Super Bowl was in my current hometown of Las Vegas.

Mom flew out and spent the week with us, and on Saturday she and I went to the auction. It was a full-day event lasting close to seven hours. All of Dad's live auction items sold. The most popular piece was his Super Bowl V ring. Once the auction had concluded, Mom and I got ready to leave. I happened to see the person who purchased the ring at the front desk. He was accompanied by two other individuals. I was debating whether or not to say anything to the man, and decided a simple thank-you would be nice. I introduced myself and said, "Thanks for buying my dad's ring."

It took a brief second for what I said to register, and then a huge smile came across his face. I told him I was John's son, and also introduced him to Mom. He introduced his two adult sons to us. It turned out that the man was from Mexico and had been a huge fan of Dad's going back to Super Bowl V in January 1971. It was the first game he had ever watched, and Dad left a lasting impression on him and, later, his sons.

Football has become such a passion for the family that the three gentlemen have attended the past fifteen Super Bowls together. He told us about his plans for building a special display box for the ring and promised to send us photos once it was completed. The man and his sons were extremely nice, and it was obvious how highly they regarded Dad. It made Mom and I feel great to know the ring was going to someone it meant so much to, and not someone who would turn around and sell it in the near future.

As we talked, I mentioned to the father that I was producing a film about Dad and offered to share the script with him if he would be interested in reading it. Since meeting at the auction, he and his sons have read the script, we have had multiple Zoom calls about the project, and they are now joining the *UNITAS* team as executive producers. I knew Dad was big in the United States, but had no clue his popularity carried over to Mexico.

I am so fortunate to have parents who raised me to be respectful and considerate of others. A simple thank-you has gotten us one step closer to moving *UNITAS* into production. Like my dad always said, "It doesn't cost anything to be nice"—and he was right!

ACKNOWLEDGMENTS

Dianna, for twenty-two years (and counting), you have been by my side. Multiple moves, a movie, and now a book. Never once have you said no, or let's not do that. You've definitely rolled your eyes a few times, but you still support me and these crazy ideas. I do not take for granted how fortunate I am to have you as my wife and mother of our children.

When Kristine Setting Clark, my coauthor, contacted me a couple of years ago about writing a book, I told her I wasn't all that interested. After all, I was in the middle of developing a screenplay and trying to raise money to make a film. The last thing I wanted to do was write more. She explained to me that she spoke with my dad multiple times about writing a book together and offered to meet him at the Pro Football Hall of Fame induction ceremony. "Honey, I don't go to the induction ceremony," was his straightforward reply.

Despite not really wanting to write a book, I told Kristine I would think about it. There had to be a reason other than just telling random stories about my personal life, which isn't all that interesting. In my mind, *the* book about Dad had already been written by Tom Callahan.

After some time, Kristine reconnected with me, and we talked further. I told her I would only be willing to write the book if we could figure out a way to piece together the lessons Dad had taught me and how I applied them to my life. These twenty lessons are the outline for how I, along with Dianna, raise our boys. They also have helped me to stay disciplined and not quit on my dream of making the *UNITAS* movie a reality. I'm glad Kristine contacted me and kept on me about writing the book. It's been an enjoyable experience. I have been able to reflect on my past and be reminded, again, just how fortunate I am to have been raised by both my dad and mom.

Even though Dad was always front and center because of who he was and what he accomplished on the football field, it was my mom who was the backbone of the family. She "steered the ship" day in and day out, and was a true role model for unconditional love and support for Paige, Chad, and me. Mom could have been very intimidated by who my dad was when they met in 1972. He was at the end of his career and had firmly established himself as one of the GOATs (greatest of all time). Obviously, she wasn't. They married in 1973 and I was born in 1974. She was always by his side, and he was by hers. There was a small sign in our home that said, "The greatest gift a father can give to his children is to love their mother." While that's true, marriage is a partnership, so the real statement should be, "The greatest gift parents can give their kids is the love they show for one another." My parents did that, and I have tried to do the same in my marriage.

I had a lot of extra academic support over the years, but the most beneficial support came from Pam Pierce. During seventh and eighth grade she helped me get ready for high school. She taught me organizational techniques that I still use to this day. She taught me study skills that made my life easier and studying more efficient. But most of all, she helped me with writing. Prior to working with Pam, writing was more of a task necessary for school; she taught me to enjoy the creative process. I learned how to brainstorm ideas and organize thoughts into comprehensive text. In ninth grade, Pam was my English teacher. Up until then, I couldn't stand reading, but she made that enjoyable as well. Interpreting the text and digging into what the author was trying to say became fun. Pam is the one teacher who really took her time with me and helped me develop as a student. For that, I am forever grateful.

I would like to thank Dan Fouts and Joe Namath for taking time to write the forewords for the book. Over the years I've heard many stories about being a teammate with Dan and competing against Joe. My dad held both of these men in high regard and was appreciative of the friendship he had with each of them.

Finally, I'd like to thank Ken Samelson and the entire team at Lyons Press and the Globe Pequot Publishing Group for giving me a chance to share these lessons, and my story. Thank you for your trust in allowing me, along with Kristine, to write *Unitas to Unitas: Life's Lessons Passed Down from Father to Son.*

References

Books

Callahan, John. *Johnny U: The Life and Times of Johnny Unitas*. New York: Crown Archetype, 2010.

Harrison, Harry H., Jr. *Father to Son: Life's Lessons on Raising a Boy*. New York: Workman Publishing Company, 2013.

Videos

Drew Brees Breaks Johnny Unitas' Record, NFL Films, 2013. https://www.neworleanssaints.com/video/nfl-films-drew-brees-breaks-johnny-unitas-record-8911005

Sports of the 20th Century: Johnny Unitas, HBO Sports and NFL Productions, written and directed by Ray Didinger and Steve Seidman, 1999. https://www.youtube.com/watch?v=9Tleop6m4E0

About the Authors

Joe Unitas is the producer and cowriter of the upcoming film *UNITAS*. The movie is a tribute to his father who taught him the values of determination and perseverance, and a work ethic that has enabled him to envision the story, cowrite the screenplay, develop the business plan, and assemble a team of industry professionals to bring his father's story to the world.

While living in Los Angeles for seven years, he had parts in five films: *Any Given Sunday*, *Raising Helen*, *Max Keeble's Big Move*, *Bandits*, and *The Princess Diaries*. During that time, he also studied and performed in plays at Playhouse West, where he was taught by Robert Carnegie and Jeff Goldblum. He lives in Las Vegas, Nevada.

Dr. Kristine Setting Clark was a longtime feature writer for the San Francisco 49ers' and Dallas Cowboys' *Gameday* magazines. She is the author of *Undefeated, Untied and Uninvited: A Documentary of the 1951 University San Francisco Dons Football Team*, *Legends of the Hall: 1950s*, and *Football's Fabulous Fifties: When Men Were Men and the Grass Was Still Real*. She has coauthored the autobiographies of Pro Football Hall of Fame members Bob St. Clair, Bob Lilly, Y. A. Tittle, Jim Taylor, Sam Huff, and Art Donovan. She also coauthored *Cheating Is Encouraged: The Oakland Raiders of the 1970s* with former Raider Mike Siani.

Dr. Clark resides in Stockton, California, and has two grown children and four grandsons. Her oldest grandson, Justin, is the godson of former 49er All-Pro and Hall of Fame member Bob St. Clair.